You can never shake

the ancient dust

of Africa

off your boots.

SAFARI

The Romance and the Reality

MOLLY BUCHANAN

with Shan & Dave Varty

Photographs by Richard du Toit

NATIONAL GEOGRAPHIC

WASHINGTON, D.C.

PAGES 2–3: *A yound leopard at Londolozi*
THIS PAGE: *An elephant in the Savuti Game Reserve mock charges a 4 x 4.*
PAGES 6–7: *a group of Samburu in the northern frontier district of Kenya*
PAGES 8–9: *Blesbok in the fynbos region of the southern Cape*
PAGES 10–11: *White pelicans in Botswana's Okavango Delta*
PAGES 12–13: *Mother giraffe and baby*
PAGES 14–15 *Springbok and blue wildebeest in the Kgalagadi Transfrontier Park, which links parks in South Africa and Botswana*

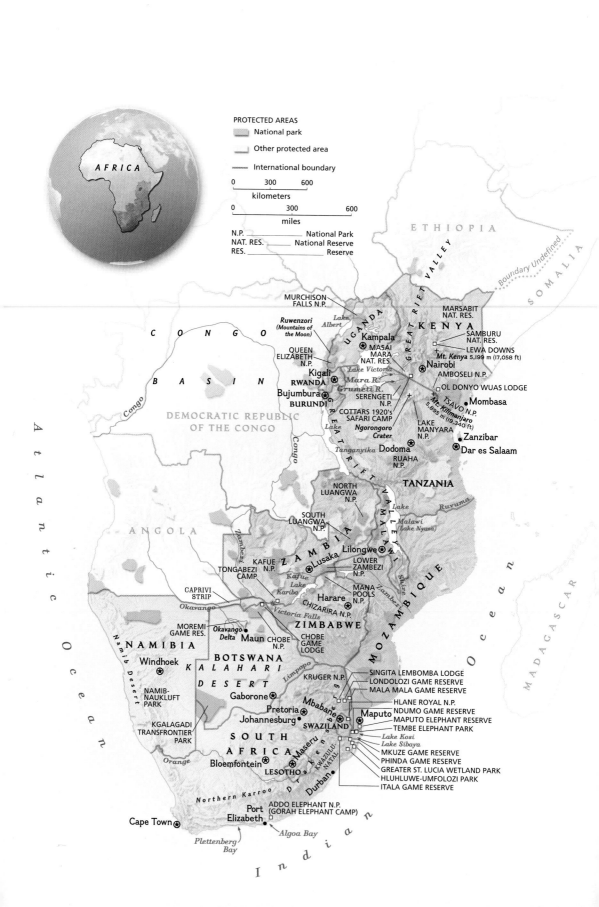

PROTECTED AREAS
National park
Other protected area
International boundary

0   300   600
kilometers

0   300   600
miles

N.P.   National Park
NAT. RES.   National Reserve
RES.   Reserve

AFRICA

CONGO

BASIN

DEMOCRATIC REPUBLIC
OF THE CONGO

ETHIOPIA

SOMALIA

Boundary Undefined

Atlantic Ocean

ANGOLA

MURCHISON
FALLS N.P.

*Ruwenzori
(Mountains of
the Moon)*

QUEEN
ELIZABETH
N.P.

Kampala

*Lake
Albert*

UGANDA

MASAI
MARA
NAT. RES.

Lake Victoria

RWANDA
Kigali

Bujumbura
BURUNDI

Mara R.
Grumeti R.
SERENGETI
N.P.

COTTARS 1920's
SAFARI CAMP

*Ngorongoro
Crater*

*Lake
Tanganyika*

Dodoma

RUAHA
N.P.

TANZANIA

KENYA

MARSABIT
NAT. RES.

SAMBURU
NAT. RES.

LEWA DOWNS

Mt. Kenya 5,199 m (17,058 ft)

Nairobi

AMBOSELI N.P.

OL DONYO WUAS LODGE

*Mt. Kilimanjaro
5,895 m (19,340 ft)*

TSAVO N.P.

Mombasa

LAKE
MANYARA
N.P.

Zanzibar

Dar es Salaam

GREAT RIFT VALLEY

GREAT RIFT VALLEY

Congo

Congo

NORTH
LUANGWA
N.P.

SOUTH
LUANGWA
N.P.

ZAMBIA

KAFUE
N.P.

TONGABEZI
CAMP

Zambezi

*Kafue
Lake
Kariba*

Lusaka

Lilongwe

LOWER
ZAMBEZI
N.P.

MANA
POOLS
N.P.

*Lake
Malawi
(Lake Nyasa)*

Ruvuma

Shire

MALAWI

MOZAMBIQUE

MADAGASCAR

Indian Ocean

CAPRIVI
STRIP

Okavango

MOREMI
GAME RES.

*Okavango
Delta*

Maun

CHOBE
N.P.

Harare

CHIZARIRA N.P.

Victoria Falls

ZIMBABWE

CHOBE
GAME
LODGE

Zambezi

Namib Desert

NAMIBIA

Windhoek

NAMIB-
NAUKLUFT
PARK

KGALAGADI
TRANSFRONTIER
PARK

BOTSWANA

KALAHARI

DESERT

Gaborone

Limpopo

KRUGER N.P.

SINGITA LEMBOMBA LODGE
LONDOLOZI GAME RESERVE
MALA MALA GAME RESERVE

HLANE ROYAL N.P.
NDUMO GAME RESERVE
MAPUTO ELEPHANT RESERVE
TEMBE ELEPHANT PARK

Lake Kosi
Lake Sibaya

MKUZE GAME RESERVE
PHINDA GAME RESERVE
GREATER ST. LUCIA WETLAND PARK
HLUHLUWE-UMFOLOZI PARK
ITALA GAME RESERVE

Pretoria
Johannesburg
SWAZILAND
Mbabane

Maputo

SOUTH

AFRICA

Maseru
LESOTHO

Drakensberg

*KWAZULU-
NATAL*

Durban

Bloemfontein

Orange

Northern Karroo

ADDO ELEPHANT N.P.
(GORAH ELEPHANT CAMP)

Port
Elizabeth

Cape Town

*Plettenberg
Bay*

Algoa Bay

Indian Ocean

Introduction

WHAT MAKES PEOPLE JOURNEY TO AFRICA? IT IS HARDLY THE HEAT AND the dust, the scorpions and the snakes. You sleep in a sweat. You wake up on full alert, all senses straining. You listen without moving a muscle. Could it have been the lilting song of the white-browed coucal, or perhaps a nightjar lifting its melody to the full moon that has disturbed your slumber? And then you hear an unmistakable rumble. An elephant is rubbing itself against your tent and there is nothing but a thin canvas between you and the largest land mammal on this planet. You hold your breath, waiting. But elephants walk gently where they are treated with respect, and long ago they learned to walk without tripping on the guy ropes of tents. The African wilderness is a place that gives you the privilege of seeing this planet as it was millions of years ago.

ABOVE: *Compass* OPPOSITE: *Africa has become a continent of borders and fences. The transfrontier park vision is to link island reserves, taking down fences and reinstating ancient migration routes.*

A dominant male impala aggressively defends his territory. After the initial horn–clashing, the intruder will often retire uninjured to fight another day, but serious injury or death can result.

Europe's fascination with Africa goes back to the days when men sought an alternative route to the East—to the diamonds of Goa, the spices of Zanzibar, and the pearls of the Orient. The overland route was blocked by the Venetians, who held a monopoly on trade between the diamond merchants of India and the gem cutters of Europe. In 1498, under the patronage of Don Manuel, king of Portugal, the route to India via the Cape was discovered. The diamond monopoly was broken and the way was open for the great explorers of central and southern Africa. At first few took up the challenge, but eventually the trickle became a stream and then a flood as people from all over the world came to Africa, not just for the diamonds, gold, and platinum, but to seek adventure, to plunder, and to make their fortunes.

What was it that created this fascination, that made people return again and again? Perhaps there is no simple answer. Africa is a paradox: a savage land, a sensitive land, a fragile land. The continent is where our journey began, where humans developed a brain-to-body ratio out of all proportion to that of any other creature in this living world. Yet it is a place where time stood still for hundreds and thousands of years. Today we might well ask if there was any need to change the lifestyle evolved by *Homo sapiens* in Africa—a lifestyle that, however harsh the checks and balances, was so perfectly adapted to the environment that it could have been sustained forever.

Africa is a continent of wild beauty, of extraordinary panoramas, of sunset and sunrise spectacles that make you gape with wonder. It can be a place of eerie silence. Or, when you find yourself in a war zone between wild dogs and hyenas or lions and elephants, the cacophony can pierce your eardrums. Great cloudbursts periodically thunder from the skies. Hail flattens everything in its path. Lightning splits huge trees in two. Then comes a time of drought, no clouds, no rain, hardly a breath of wind, only relentless heat and dust day after day. Africa is a place of continually unfolding drama: Life and death are center stage, woven together in nature's gigantic tapestry. Africa gives us a broad hint of the complexity of creation, and shows us the hand of the creator.

The word "safari" came to East Africa with the Arab dhows that sailed down the coast in search of gold, ivory, and slaves. It means a journey, and there are two journeys one makes when one comes to Africa. One is all spectacle and adrenaline, magnificence and excitement. The other is an inner journey of the soul. Unconsciously we discover an affinity with Africa, perhaps because in the cradle of mankind we discover our roots.

In the past 200 years much has been written on Africa. This story touches here and there on the lives of people who are making an impact on the conservation of Africa's heritage of wildlife. Going on safari allows us to reconnect our busy lives to our extraordinary and beautiful planet. In Africa the web of nature is apparent; we can see how species interact with one another in their struggle for survival. There is no denying that life is tough. But one thing is clear in Africa: We cannot ignore the awesome forces of nature. We have to learn to coexist with her. We need to start somewhere and learn. Africa, so closely linked to nature, is a good place to begin.

Prologue

THE AIR WAS HOT AND STILL. *NOW AND THEN THE SILENCE OF THE BUSHVELD would be broken. Perhaps a bird would call or a twig would snap. But the silence would close in again and it seemed impossible that this dried-out landscape could support wildlife. Dave Varty was in despair. He had watched the distressed hippo population in the river—the river that all his life had flowed with crystal-clear water. It was an artery that brought life to the bushveld—that peculiar mix of trees and grasslands that feeds the great herds of Africa. Now, for the first time in living memory, the river had stopped flowing. The hippos were dying. If the rains did not come soon, many other animals would die.*

ABOVE: *Warthog skull* OPPOSITE: *A display of the dominant bull hippo's large tusklike canines is often enough to send off neighboring territorial bulls or bring younger males to order.*

These lions were part of a coalition of four brothers that banded together to protect their pride and their territory from neighboring lions in the Kwai River area of Botswana.

When Dave arrived back at his home on the banks of the Sand River in Londolozi, his wife, Shan, turned to him: "Enos just called. He said a friend had just been released from prison. Could we look after him and tell him about conservation?" "Why," wondered Dave, "Why would Enos want us to tell this story to an ex-prisoner?" Then Shan added: "His name is Nelson. Nelson Mandela."

Dave Varty and Enos Mabuza, Chief Minister of KaNgwane, the neighboring district, had found each other across the great divide of apartheid. They had become friends and for more than a decade had shared ideas while out in the bush together. Dave would say, "the Swiss have watches and mountains. We have the bushveld and the animals. All we are doing is destroying the very assets that should be the backbone of our economy. We should be taking care of our land, our wildlife, and our people. That is my model for the future."

"A few days after Enos called, Nelson Mandela arrived, alone," remembers Dave. "From the moment he stepped out of the helicopter and I shook hands with him I knew I was in the presence of a man of extraordinary vitality. We set off in an open Land Rover on what was to be Madiba's (as he had become affectionately known) first ever game drive and one of the defining moments of my life. We did not talk much. We needed to settle into the rhythm of our surroundings. I also had my work cut out, as I was both driver and tracker. Almost immediately, a leopard crossed the road ahead of us and disappeared into the dense bush. I could see she was hunting. We followed off-road as she darted this way and that, following every twist and turn of her prey. Madiba never said a word. Here, I had the opportunity to show him the great theater of Africa. And as the tension mounted, she took the impala right in front of us, killed and fed for a while, and then hoisted her prize into a tree. As the drama ended I began to explain the model for conservation we had developed at Londolozi. I knew that at last a great listener had arrived—and that this man would make a profound difference to conservation in Africa.

"On the way home I talked. I told him the experience we had just had was far more than a moment of excitement. The wildlife of Africa could create jobs for people and reduce poverty in rural areas. I told him of the model of care we had developed and that here was an opportunity for ecotourism. I went on to explain that the wildlife of the Kruger Park and its adjacent private reserves would be destroyed if too much water in the rivers was used upstream. Eventually Nelson said to me: 'Dave, when we run this country we will not permit the river catchments to be abused. I promise you, we will bring appropriate management to the rivers. We will expand the parks. We will create more space for wildlife. Africa's people will benefit.'"

Dave had no need to worry about whether Mandela would remember his promise. A few months after his visit, Dave was asked to host five members of the African National Congress (ANC), one of whom was Thabo Mbeki, Mandela's great ally and eventual successor as president of South Africa. Mandela was elected president in 1994. After that, under the direction of Professor Kader Asmal, Minister of Water Affairs and Forestry, river management started to improve—as did legislation relating to tourism and the environment. Former U.S. Secretary of the Interior Bruce Babbitt has described South Africa's National Water Conservation Campaign as "unprecedented in terms of its approach and effectiveness, anywhere in the world."

The Vartys' Londolozi Game Reserve was in many respects an example of what was to happen, or had happened, in many parts of Africa. Land had been damaged and degraded by humans, and animals had disappeared, but Londolozi had found solutions. The result is that today it has all the ingredients that are considered essential for a successful safari: abundant wildlife and wilderness landscapes of great beauty, peace, and romance.

Chapter One

The Changing Face of Africa

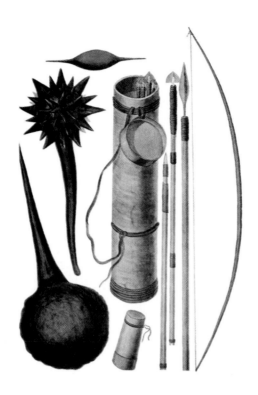

*A*S THE HOT GOLDEN ORB DISAPPEARED BEHIND THE CLOUDS ON THE *horizon, giant rays of light spread across the western sky. The colors changed from blues to purples and pinks and from gold to peach and orange, and the shining crescent of a new moon, like a cupped hand, appeared in the velvety sky, with Venus, the brilliant evening star, poised above. Far in the distance a lion roared. It was time to hunt. It was an evening in Africa that could have been a thousand years ago. But so much had changed.*

ABOVE: *Sketches of Khoikhoi weapons by François Levaillant*
OPPOSITE: *Zulu Prince Dabulamanzi, 1879* PRECEDING PAGES: *The extinct quagga*

Over the past two centuries human populations on the African continent have escalated from some 50 million to 840 million. More significant is that although it took 100,000 years to reach the first 50 million, the population has grown by more than 500 million over the past 40 years. Some say that wildlife should give way to agriculture, to provide more food for hungry mouths. But the pressure of increasing numbers of farmers on semiarid regions is having serious consequences on land more suited to wildlife than to cattle and cultivation. Only about 8 percent of the continent is arable and free of nagana, the cattle disease carried by the tsetse fly. Thousands of people are facing starvation because so much of the land has been drained of nutrients, and the water table that was once just below the surface has dropped out of reach of much of the vegetation.

Ken Tinley, the ecologist who guided Dave Varty and his brother John in the rejuvenation of Londolozi, said that Africa's greatest paradox is that people are dying amid plenty. He advocated a policy of "maximum sustainable utilization" of the wilderness and insisted that rural people should be reconnected to the benefits of the land. The continent has some 90 different antelope and other hoofed species, a far greater protein resource than that possessed by any other continent. This natural resource is almost completely untapped, with the exceptions of ostrich and spring-bok, which have flourished in the past decade as a result of sustainable ranching.

South Africa, one of the first African countries to decimate its wildlife through uncontrolled hunting, is now leading the way in restoring wildlife pop-ulations and developing models for the sustainable use of indigenous resources. There is no doubt that Africa could be the ecotourism destination of the world. The might of the Zambezi River in full flood, pouring over the chasm of the Victoria Falls, is breathtaking. The grasslands of the Serengeti and the Masai Mara, dotted with millions of wildebeest, zebra, gazelle, impala, and other ani-mals, are awe-inspiring. Every moment following a Londolozi leopard on the hunt is charged with excitement. The snowcapped equatorial peaks of Kilimanjaro, Mount Kenya, and the Mountains of the Moon are sublime in their splendor. The land of water—the Okavango Delta—is a verdant wetland surrounded by desert. The amazing coral reefs and pristine beaches of Africa's eastern coast-line rival coral reefs and beaches anywhere in the world.

Once the decision is made that we want to keep this beauty for future gener-ations, we have to get down to work, first to understand what is happening to the land and the wildlife and then to find solutions to the problems facing Africa's people. Of one thing we are certain: The fates of both are inextricably bound. There is a Zulu proverb that says, "To go forward we must first look back."

"The koodoo," or kudu, drawn, engraved, and published in London by Samuel Daniell in 1804

IT SEEMS FAR-FETCHED TO SUGGEST that Napoleon was the key to change in Africa. But his brilliance on the battlefield acted as a catalyst to accelerate scientific advances in every aspect of gunnery. The weapons used by the early explorers to Africa had made little impact against the often-aggressive tribes or the formidable wild animals. Men came and they took little. However, by the mid-19th century weapons were more accurate and, with breech loading, far more efficient. When Europeans arrived with these modern guns they also brought shovels and plows. With their arrival, Africa was drawn into a downward spiral of exploitation and degradation that seemed unstoppable.

At the end of the 19th century the dominant European countries (Britain, Germany, France, Belgium, Spain, Holland, Italy, and Portugal) had divided up the continent of Africa. The full impact of these decisions only became apparent a half century later, when the newly independent countries started to confront their colonial legacy.

Africa had its own defense mechanisms against invaders: The tsetse fly spread cattle disease and also carried sleeping sickness, and various species of mosquito

ABOVE: *Blue buck, which became extinct in about 1800* RIGHT: *Bushpigs, which survived, and, in the background, Cape mountain lions, which did not*

carried yellow fever and malaria. Until the discovery of the insecticidal properties of DDT during World War II, these diseases provided natural barriers where they occurred—tsetse fly in the drier wood-lands and scrublands, and mosquitoes in the hot, wet areas.

For more than two centuries after Portuguese ships had traced the complete outline of the African continent, the Cape coast was left largely undisturbed. The whales came into the bays to drop their calves, and the lagoons reflected the magnificent mountain ranges and forests. Inland, the plains turned white with congregations of springbok, and elephants continued to wander back and forth in their quest for food and water. But changes were in the pipeline. Almost a cen-tury after the Dutch challenged the Portuguese seafaring nation and established a settlement at the Cape in 1652, farmers began to spread farther and farther afield in their search for well-watered land and plentiful game.

Baron Joachim van Plettenberg, Governor of the Cape of Good Hope from 1774 to 1785, was one of the first dignitaries to journey a long distance inland. In the company of Robert Jacob Gordon, who commanded the Dutch East India

Company's armed forces at the Cape, he set off in 1778 to inspect the northern and eastern frontier districts, traveling by coach over some of the most hazardous mountain tracks imaginable. Perhaps it was the baron who, disdaining the discomforts of travel and maintaining his elegance and discerning taste for fine wines, set the standard for future safaris in Africa.

A few years later 27-year-old François Levaillant, who had been born in Dutch Guiana, interrupted his voyage to France, stopping at the Cape of Good Hope. The young man was totally fascinated by nature, which, as he expressed it, "deigned to be my first instructor." His few years in Africa gave him a wealth of material that occupied him for the next 30 years. He was a prolific recorder although he was wont to exaggerate—particularly about his own skills. Of his first elephant hunt he wrote that as "night was drawing on, we happened to find the elephant which I had the good fortune to kill with a single shot"—quite an achievement in 1781, almost a century before gunnery became efficient.

Levaillant was an incurable romantic, writing of a young Hottentot woman whom he renamed Narina (which in her language signified a flower): "the most sparkling gems were not so brilliant as her expressive eyes." He then gave her name to one of the most gorgeous birds in southern Africa, the Narina trogon, a brilliant shimmering red-and-green bird. Klaas, his loyal and trusted servant, became immortalized when Levaillant gave the name Klaas's cuckoo to a beautiful iridescent-green bird.

Explorers such as Levaillant, Sir Richard Burton, Sir Samuel Baker, and Henry Morton Stanley, all endowed with the ability to paint, draw, and write expressively, set in motion a passion to journey to Africa to see landscapes so dazzling and wildlife so diverse and magnificent that there was nothing to compare anywhere in the known world. Added to that, the journey had much to offer that was lacking in the lives of young men at that time. There was excitement and danger and the thrill of new discoveries. There was the opportunity to be recognized by the Royal Geographical Society, to be knighted for geographical services, and, for those in the army, to be promoted to higher ranks.

The 19th century was a busy period in the exploration of Africa and led to the publication of numerous books and periodicals. One popular publication of the time, written by Capt. William Cornwallis Harris and entitled *The Wild Sports of Southern Africa,* was republished five times in a little over a decade. Cornwallis Harris spent a decade in India with the British army before transferring in 1836 to the Cape, where it was intended that he recuperate from ill health. Such was his excitement on arriving at the Cape that he wasted no time in setting off on a two-year safari. In his book, he wrote of "the vast herds of zebras, gnoos, sassaybes, and hartebeests pouring down from every quarter until the landscape literally presented the appearance of a moving mass of game."

Cornwallis Harris was followed by other men who made their mark in southern Africa and who arrived with devastating weapons: R. Gordon Cumming arrived in 1843, William Charles Baldwin in 1851, and Frederick Courteney

OPPOSITE: *François Levaillant's illustrations of his loyal Khoikhoi servants, Narina and Klaas, and the two birds to which he gave their names: the Narina trogon and Klaas's cuckoo*
FOLLOWING PAGES: *"The African rhinoceros" by Samuel Daniell*

Selous in 1871. All three were hunters of extraordinary courage and all published accounts of their adventures. Perhaps the most famous of all the legendary names to hunt in Africa was Selous. Theodore Roosevelt, who hired Selous as his guide on his epic safari to East Africa in 1909, described him as a man of "untiring energy and fearless intention," and "a man whose humility was always as conspicuous as his bravery."

Another traveler to Africa was Thomas Baines, a prolific artist who completed more than 4,000 paintings and sketches of superb quality between his arrival in South Africa in 1842 and his death in Durban in 1875. His safaris included an abortive expedition in 1857 with Dr. David Livingstone up the Zambezi to the Morumba rapids—a discovery that put an end to Livingstone's belief that the Zambezi would be the gateway to the interior. Baines was the first artist to capture the Victoria Falls on canvas.

The year of Baines's death marked the arrival at the Cape of another man who was to influence generations of young men. The six years that Rider Haggard spent in Africa provided the material for numerous romantic tales of its land, its people, and its wildlife. His fictional character Allan Quatermain, based on Selous, was a 19th-century equivalent of James Bond. Quatermain, with his unlimited daring and courage, launched many an African safari and became the hero of 14 novels and several films including *King Solomon's Mines,* starring Stewart Granger and Deborah Kerr, and *She,* with Helen Douglas and Randolph Scott.

Even as writers and artists such as Thomas Baines and Rider Haggard painted and recorded their stories, the plains of southern Africa were changing dramatically. The huge herds that once covered the landscape from horizon to horizon were disappearing under a heavy barrage of indiscriminate hunting. The elephants that had wandered between the mountains and the plains of the Cape had long since disappeared. The sound of guns had driven those in the east into the dense coastal forests. To the west they escaped into the dry desert. By the 1860s the blue buck, quagga, and Cape lion had been shot into extinction. Thereafter commercial hunting quickly mopped up what was left of the wildlife and put an end to hunting safaris in the Cape. Before the start of the 20th century no hippo remained south of the Orange River. And had it not been for Mr. Ford and his invention of the automobile, giraffe would have disappeared entirely. Their long skins were used to inspan oxen—the only means of transporting goods in that era. The wildlife that had evolved over millions of years was being wiped out in a hundred.

*A stylized picture of leopard and cheetah by Capt. William Cornwallis Harris,
who traveled and hunted all over South Africa in 1836 and 1837*

Another extraordinary character emerged in Natal at this time. John Dunn was orphaned in 1851 at the age of 17. A charging elephant had killed his father, and his mother, whose father and brothers had been killed in 1838 when Dingane, king of the Zulus, invaded Natal, died soon thereafter. Dunn was left with little but his wits, an ox wagon, and, when he was still in his teens, a young wife. He was a capable young man, not only fluent in the Zulu language but also familiar with Zulu customs. He became a trusted adviser to the future Zulu king, Cetshwayo, and within a few decades amassed a household of 48 Zulu wives, which gave him easy access to Zulu territory. He also formed a private army of a hundred men whom he trained in the arts of hunting, especially for the most profitable prey of all—elephants. Once again, a pattern of destruction had been set in motion. A mere 76 years after the first settler, Henry Francis Fynn, arrived in Durban in 1824, the elephants of Natal had disappeared.

Lord Randolph Churchill undertook one of the last grand safaris to southern Africa in 1892. Leaving his young son, Winston, at home devouring Rider Haggard's adventures, to which he was addicted, Lord Randolph journeyed through the Cape to Mashonaland, present-day Zimbabwe, with a caravan of four heavy Cape wagons and several smaller wagons and carts. His party consisted of a professional hunter, a surgeon, four cooks, a police officer, an army

safari manager, and hundreds of drivers and attendants. He even traveled with a piano, cans of meat, and the ubiquitous jeroboams of champagne.

By the start of the 20th century the destruction of game in South Africa was virtually complete. Lt. Col. James Stevenson-Hamilton, a Scot who had come to South Africa with the British Army, was appointed the first game warden of the Sabi Game Reserve in 1902. This reserve, later consolidated into the Kruger National Park, was dubbed "the gameless game reserve." There were no elephants, white rhino, or eland left, and only a handful of buffalo had survived the hunters and the rinderpest epidemic of 1896. Five giraffe remained, while antelope had been virtually annihilated by the "biltong" (dried meat) hunters. Stevenson-Hamilton wrote that it was the general opinion at the time that "wild animals existed to be killed with as much profit as possible to the killer." There were no hunting ethics whatsoever. If a man did not succeed in killing the animal he had fired at, the next best thing, for his own glorification, was to have wounded it. Stevenson-Hamilton proposed a war on poachers and all "vermin"—principally lions, leopards, cheetahs, and wild dogs—in order to restore the plains herds that had been so depleted.

In 1908 Stevenson-Hamilton visited Kenya, and his path crossed with that of Theodore Roosevelt. It was a major event in his life and led, through discussion and subsequent correspondence, to the publication in 1910 of his book *Animal Life in Africa*, with a foreword written by the President. The American influence continued and Stevenson-Hamilton made many references to Yellowstone National Park during his war to preserve wildlife in the face of huge opposition from hunters and farmers. From Roosevelt he learned about the founding of Yellowstone National Park on a wave of national pride. Following this example, he suggested that the new reserve be named after President Paul Kruger, the founder of Afrikaner nationalism. This proposal finally defused political opposition, and in 1926 the Kruger National Park was proclaimed.

Over the centuries the style of the safari has changed dramatically: François Levaillant's ox wagons and Roosevelt's line of porters, each loaded to the hilt and with paraffin lamps swinging rhythmically to their footsteps, have given way to the modern-day private jet that wings its way into the heart of the African wilderness. The overlying focus of the safari has also changed: from exploration to hunting to shooting film. What has not changed is the instinctive desire to connect with the ancient rhythms of nature, still prevalent in Africa.

TOP ROW: *Commodore butterflies* CENTER ROW: *two Charaxes, two Catopsilia* BOTTOM ROW: *Swordtail, Swallowtail* FOLLOWING PAGES: *"Scene in Sitsikamma" by Samuel Daniell*

Chapter Two

The Hunting Era

FOR 340 YEARS AFTER THE FIRST EUROPEANS ROUNDED THE CAPE, THE interior of the continent remained "as mysterious as the surface of the moon" until, using quinine to control malarial fever, in 1841 David Livingstone led the way in discovering what lay beyond Africa's inhospitable coastline. For the next 32 years his objective was to find routes that would open up Africa and put an end to the slave trade that continued to flourish under the aegis of the Sultan of Zanzibar

ABOVE: *Bullets* OPPOSITE: *Princess Alice was granddaughter of Queen Victoria and wife of the Earl of Athlone, who was appointed governor general of South Africa in 1924.* PRECEDING PAGES: *Until the discovery of plastics, elephant tusks supplied the world with piano keys, billiard balls, dice, and door handles.*

long after slavery was abolished in Europe. Between 1853 and 1856 he followed the Zambezi River, reaching the Victoria Falls in 1855. In 1859 he discovered Lake Nyasa. Richard Burton and John Hanning Speke discovered Lake Tanganyika in 1858, and Speke, on his own, continued to the shores of Lake Victoria, guessing that this vast expanse of water was the source of the Nile. Henry Morton Stanley, after finding Livingstone in 1871, went on to explore the Congo. The way was open for the colonialists and then for the safaris to East Africa, the Zambezi Valley, and beyond to the Congo, Botswana, and Angola.

Theodore Roosevelt's safari in 1909 was the first great safari to East Africa. His journey had much in common with those undertaken by François

ABOVE: *Policemen tried to enforce antipoaching laws after proclamation of the Sabi Game Reserve in 1898.* LEFT: *Before the land was crisscrossed with fences, zebras could move freely during droughts.* FOLLOWING PAGES: *The red line on a map by Henry Lichtenstein shows the route taken by Joachim van Plettenberg in 1778 on what must have been one of the first safaris in Africa.*

Levaillant in the 1780s. Both men observed wildlife keenly, collected specimens for scientific institutions, and took great pleasure in the challenge of hunting on foot in the wildest areas of Africa. Both men also had a passion for the natural world and published highly readable accounts of their African adventures. It was sportsmen hunters such as Roosevelt, who played a major role in the conservation of land in the United States, who were the instigators and the driving force behind the establishment of game reserves in Africa. Another example was James Stevenson-Hamilton, who put his energies into fighting a war against poachers and who, in the face of considerable opposition from land-hungry farmers, succeeded in having the Kruger National Park proclaimed. Others included Charles Varty and Frank Unger, who were the first to buy a private hunting estate in South Africa. They were followed by Wac Campbell, who became their neighbor on Mala Mala a year later. If you had asked any of these men whether they were hunters or conservationists, they would have given an unequivocal reply: "Both."

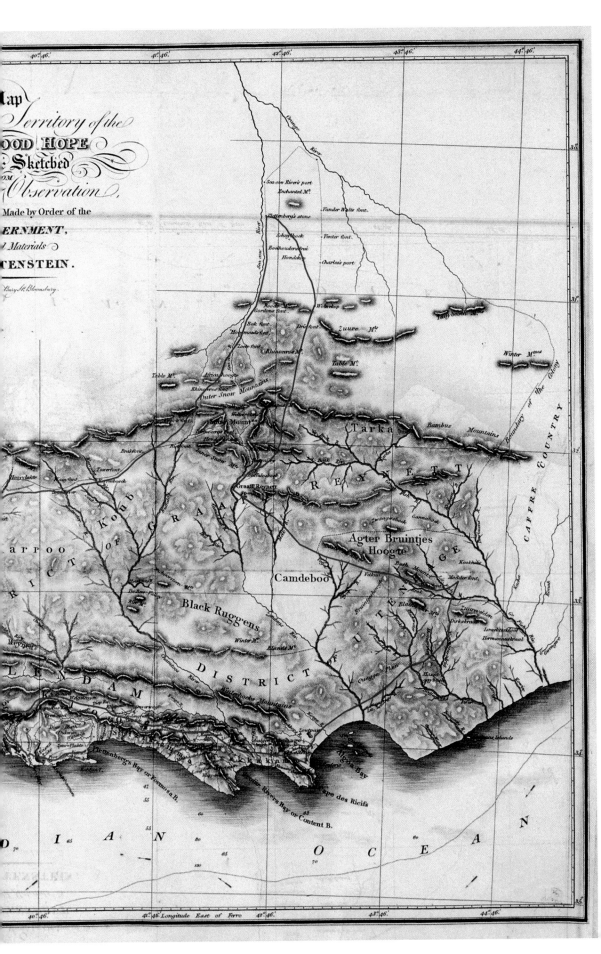

With the arrival of the professional hunter and the record book there was, however, a major change in emphasis. Size became all-important and statistics the ultimate measure of achievement. In the headlong search for trophies, the animals carrying the best genes were placed under pressure: the elephant with the biggest tusks, the kudu with the longest spiraling horns, the rhino with the greatest upturned horns. The result is that elephants whose tusks are comparable with the massive Kenya record of tusks weighing 225 and 210 pounds each are unlikely ever to be seen again.

There were also men employed to clear land of game to make way for agriculture. J. A. Hunter was given the task of preparing land south of the Chyulu Hills, between Amboseli and Tsavo. After he shot 994 rhinoceros he wrote: "Is it worth killing off these strange and marvelous animals just to clear a few more acres for people that are ever on the increase? I don't know. But I know this. The time will come when there is no more land to be cleared. What will be done then?" Prophetic words.

FOR THOUSANDS OF YEARS THE PEOPLE OF AFRICA lived in equilibrium with their environment, never taking more than the Earth could provide. They were hunter-gatherers, whose sole objective was to acquire food. In doing so, they developed a wisdom and understanding of the laws of nature that are still with us today. Winnis Mathebula, who was entrusted with the care of Dave and John Varty, was one example. He had come to their farm in 1926 and had stayed to guide three generations of the Varty family until his death. "Winnis was a hunter-gatherer of a bygone era," remembers Dave. "When the colonialists arrived people like Winnis were labeled poachers and jailed for breaking the law. Winnis had taken a job in the Kruger National Park and his outstanding abilities as a tracker were soon evident. But he was accused of killing an impala and he lost his job. Fortunately Harry Kirkman, warden of the Sabi Sand Reserve, heard the story and was sympathetic. When my grandfather arrived...the ranger recommended that he take Winnis on."

Dave recalls, "Winnis could never wrap his mind around the changes that took place. He would shake his head in wonder when we put away our rifles and brought out cameras. Why would we spend all our time tracking—and when we did catch up with the lions, why did we not shoot? He had been a

Kilimanjaro dominates the view from the Ol Donyo Wuas Lodge in the Chyulu Hills.

great teacher and had enormous courage but little time for cowards and fools. He was a great raconteur and would often recount the tale of how one of his friends, Tie, tried to shoot a charging lion at 20 yards—and left the safety catch on! Tie fell flat on his face as the lion leapt, and neighboring farmer Stephen Roche was quick to discharge his gun. Tie's only injury was to his pride. On one occasion, when Winnis was guide to a hunting party, he called the Earl of Athlone "a bloody fool" when he missed a kudu at close range. Princess Alice, a granddaughter of Queen Victoria and wife of the earl, who was governor general of South Africa, was much amused. She had been annoyed when the men leading her hunting party would not allow her to follow a lion she had wounded. Warden Harry Kirkman tracked the lion, crawling through dense bush on Londolozi where he finally dispatched the injured animal. Although no record has been kept, the story told by the local people is that she had her way and followed Harry through the bush that now bears her name. It is still a favorite haunt of lions."

Princess Alice was considered one of the most beautiful women of her day. Her fragile beauty belied a remarkable courage and stamina and a spirit of adventure that knew no bounds. When she and her husband left South Africa in January 1931, they set off from Cape Town to Pretoria and then traveled northward through the

Continued on page 58

Mr. Roosevelt and buffalo cow in papyrus grass

Mr. Roosevelt and his son Kermit display the horns of a giant eland.

SOON AFTER HIS EPIC SAFARI TO AFRICA, THEODORE ROOSEVELT wrote: "On March 23, 1909, I sailed from New York, in charge of a scientific expedition sent out by the Smithsonian, to collect birds, mammals, reptiles, and plants, but especially specimens of big game, for the National Museum in Washington." En route to Mombasa, Roosevelt and his son Kermit met Frederick Courteney Selous, whom he described as "the greatest of the world's big-game hunters." He was to discover that Selous did not exaggerate the dangers that hunting big game posed.

Preparing a hippopotamus skin for shipment

The first bull elephant

A herd of elephants in an open forest of high timber

Mr. Roosevelt with his big bull rhino

The party traveled through Kenya, making detours to take in Kilimanjaro and Mount Kenya, and southwest to the Masai Mara. They then crossed Lake Victoria, stepping ashore at Entebbe near the Rippon Falls and the White Nile. From there the party traveled through wild Uganda country amid herds of buffalo and elephants. Soon thereafter the party sailed down the Nile to Khartoum. Roosevelt had been captivated by the thrills of the hunt but was aware of the need for conservation of a land "unworn by man." He wrote: "It is a never-ending pleasure to gaze at the great herds of buck as they move to and fro in their myriads; as they stand for their noontime rest in the quivering heat haze; as the long files come down to drink at the watering places; as they feed and fight and rest and make love."

Two Kikuyu boys, first elephant camp

Mr. Roosevelt and Kermit

Continued from page 51

heart of Africa by rail, road, and river. They visited the "high-spots" of Africa: the Victoria Falls, Kilimanjaro, Lake Victoria, the Ruwenzoris, and the Congo, and then proceeded down the White Nile by paddle steamer to the Sudan and Egypt. The first flying safaris had already begun, but Princess Alice preferred to travel by land, where she could meet people and enjoy the spectacular wildlife of Africa.

In the early years of the 20th century a hunting safari was no armchair journey even if cases of champagne were considered de rigueur. Traveling over rough terrain was extremely tough and dangerous. Describing the life of a hunter, Robert Ruark wrote that they "will walk an average of ten [miles]s over mountains and through swamps, and they will crawl from one to five miles on their bellies. If you are hunting elephants you will walk from 20 to 30 miles a day over dry river beds that suck your shoes into the sliding softness and make every step a mighty effort." Beryl Markham wrote, "The essence of elephant-hunting is discomfort in such lavish proportions that only the wealthy can afford it."

Beryl Markham was a woman of extraordinary vitality. She had been brought up by her father on a farm outside Nairobi. Her friends were local Kikuyu children, and she was more at home all her life in the wilds of Africa than at the sophisticated cocktail parties of Kenya's social elite. Two of her friends were Denys Finch Hatton and Swedish baron Bror Blixen, both portrayed in the film *Out of Africa*. Both men were professional hunters of considerable note and numbered among their clients the Prince of Wales, who took the throne of England as King Edward VIII soon after his safari to East Africa in the 1920s. Shortly before Denys was killed he had talked to Beryl about using aircraft to assist in spotting game for hunting safaris. It was a conversation she remembered, and a few years later, despite the danger of flying over extremely rough country with few places to land and even fewer signposts, she added the job of "elephant spotter" to her freelance flying operations in East Africa.

On one occasion Bror Blixen, or Blix, as his friends called him, was marooned with his client between two flooding rivers on the plains to the east of Mount Kenya. Beryl landed and took off three times on a makeshift runway that Blix cut out of the bush. It was just wide enough and long enough—with not a yard to spare—to land her airplane. Blix had no doubt about her ability to extricate the party and bring food to his African staff. She, for her part, had no doubt about his abilities either: "He never missed what he shot at," she wrote. Even then she

TOP ROW: *Long-horn wood-boring beetle, Dung beetle*
CENTER ROW: *Jewel beetle, Butterfly* BOTTOM ROW: *Moon moth, Leafhopper*

had the most terrifying experience of her life with Blix, when they were charged to within a few yards by an angry elephant. Blix had no intention of shooting the animal: He had a job to do and he wanted to keep the best tusks for his client. She wrote that Blix, in a really tight spot, became the exact opposite of the "calm, cool, and collected" hunter. He would explode, heaping expletives on his adversary—be it elephant or lion—with such passion and rapidity that the animal would be cowed.

Hunting in East Africa provided a sustainable living for many professional hunters, their crews, and the safari industry that grew up around the demand. However, hunting was banned in Uganda in 1976, and a year later in Kenya. Tony Dyer, president of the East African Professional Hunters' Association, talked to me at his home north of Mount Kenya as we watched a herd of elephants make their way across his farm into Lewa Downs. He remembers the heyday of hunting in East Africa, when the reserves and private lands teemed with wildlife. "There is no certainty as to why this decision was taken," he told us. "It could have been pressure from outside the country from one or more of the many altruistic bodies prepared to finance projects in Kenya. Many people regard hunting as a short route to the decimation of all wildlife. No one could have anticipated that the ban would have the opposite effect."

Richard Bonham and his wife, Tara, own the Ol Donyo Wuas Lodge in the Chyulu Hills overlooking the plain below Kilimanjaro, where they lease traversing rights over a 300,000-acre Masai ranch. Richard remembers: "When the hunters moved out, the poachers moved in. Nearly 90 percent of Kenya's elephants were slaughtered in the following decade. Today 10 percent of the wildlife remains that was here 25 years ago, and only a quarter of that is in proclaimed reserves. The balance is on privately owned lands, largely held by the Masai."

Richard says: "Licensed hunting can create a buffer and also an income for the landowner. Because the Masai and their cattle coexist with dangerous animals, we are frequently asked by them to take out a recalcitrant buffalo or a lion that has become too much of a danger. Often the Masai take matters into their own hands. In the last three months 5 lions have been poisoned in our area—possibly as many as 40 are poisoned over a year. These animals could earn significant funds for the Masai if they were shot under license." Richard's was not a lone voice. Nearly everyone in Kenya to whom we spoke advocated the reinstatement of hunting as a means of maintaining the country's unique heritage of wildlife.

The Maasailand Preservation Trust, set up by the Bonhams to try to make a difference in the area, receives no government support. The Bonhams have the backing of a few committed supporters and also receive donations from guests at their 16-bed lodge. These help finance the operations of the trust, which provides, among other things, a clinic and schooling for the Masai community. Richard says: "If the rural community does not derive sufficient benefit from wildlife to compensate for their losses, the wildlife will have to give way. The animals will be replaced by agriculture, which will prove to be unsustainable on this marginal land." And it is marginal. Most of the area is covered by weathered lava from relatively recent volcanic activity. The result is that rainwater drains through the porous layers of lava until it reaches base rock. The water then flows underground in a southerly direction until it bubbles up to the surface at Mzima Springs in the Tsavo National Park.

It is hard to imagine a wilderness as beautiful as the Chyulu Hills. Kilimanjaro, with its crown of snow and ice, dominates the landscape—one of the greatest elevations from plain to peak in the world. The elephants and eland have well-established paths through the hills, and the long-necked gerenuks stand on their hind legs to feed on pods of whistling thorn. Wherever one looks the bird life is spectacular: A pair of Nubian woodpeckers start to chip a cavity in a dead tree trunk; colorful little bee-eaters line up nearby like pegs on a wash line; white-headed buffalo weavers, with their brilliant orange-red patches, flit about; and their more dowdy companions, the white-bellied go-away birds, screech their warning—*go-a-waaay*.

The end of the hunting era in Kenya and Uganda coincided with increased and indiscriminate commercial poaching. In Uganda the situation was exacerbated by civil wars, which wiped out all wildlife outside national parks and over 95 percent inside the parks. The challenge for the wildlife authorities of both countries is that the suspension of hunting has forced the development of other conservation models that specifically legislate against hunting. Despite many recent efforts to lobby for a change in legislation to allow limited and controlled hunting, the antihunting resolve remains firm. Hunting is allowed in Tanzania and is a huge industry there, coexisting with tourism. However, there are signs that hunting is being mismanaged in Tanzania, leading to severe overutilization in certain areas and adding weight to the anti-hunting lobbies, which claim that the natural resources of Kenya and Uganda would suffer a similar fate and are already too far depleted.

FOLLOWING PAGES: *Game rangers in the Kruger National Park escort visitors on game trails.*
They walk for three or four days, returning to remote wilderness camps each evening.

THE HUNTING ERA

Chapter Three

Behind the Scenes

FROM 1900 ONWARD, MUCH OF AFRICA'S WILDLIFE CONTINUED ON A downward spiral. It was a story of the disappearing grasslands of the Karoo in South Africa that once teemed with springbok; of the jackal and cheetah of Namibia that had to compete with sheep farming; of the black and white rhinos that came close to extinction from the Cape to Kenya; of the pressure on the Serengeti and the Masai Mara as a result of overutilization; of the puku in Zambia's Kafue National Park, destroyed to provide money and food for an army; of the elephants of Mozambique and Tsavo—too rich a prize to be left by poachers—and of the gorillas of Rwanda that found themselves in a war zone.

ABOVE: *Cape white-eye's nest* OPPOSITE: *Dancing grey-crowned cranes* PRECEDING PAGES: *At a sanctuary in Namibia, cheetahs are rescued from the snares and bullets of farmers and relocated.*

Formal legislation to protect wildlife often came late, as it did in South Africa with the proclamation of the Kruger National Park in 1926 and the Addo Elephant National Park in 1931, by which time there were few animals left. During the colonial years many reserves were established in other parts of Africa. For the most part, these reserves have remained sanctuaries for wildlife, while outside the reserves, where there was no formal protection, the biodiversity was devastated. At the heart and soul of this tale are the people who have struggled to conserve wildlife in these remote and unprotected areas.

In the 1950s Bernard Grzimek and his son, Michael, went to Tanganyika to study the Serengeti. They brought a new dimension to wildlife management, introducing scientific systems and the powerful medium of film to communicate their story. They were the first to utilize aerial surveys to monitor wildlife populations and habitats. In South Africa James Stevenson-Hamilton made a profound difference with the securing of the Kruger National Park, and Ian Player made a huge impact on the fate of black and white rhinos, both of which faced extinction. In Kenya George Adamson, Bill Woodley, Peter Jenkins, and David Sheldrick are a few among many who contributed to wildlife conservation.

Following a different but no less committed path were a host of colorful safari operators who kept the romance and adventure of Africa alive: the Cottar family in the Masai Mara; Geoffrey Kent, who formed Abercrombie & Kent; the veteran professional hunters who formed Ker and Downey; the Campbells and Rattrays at Mala Mala—the first private photographic safari destination in Africa; the Vartys at Londolozi; and Luke Bailes at Singita. There were also the Craig family at Lewa Downs, who converted their cattle ranch to wildlife; Conservation Corporation Africa, which brought together corporate finance and conservation and built Phinda Game Reserve out of derelict farmland; Jonathan Gibson, who founded the Caprivi Conservancy at Chobe; Heinz Kohrs, who helped create the Pongolo Game Reserve in KwaZulu-Natal; Ian Hunter, who, with others, is bringing the eastern Cape wilderness back to life; and Colin Bell of Wilderness Safaris, who began a quiet revolution of the Botswana safari business.

Grasslands of the Serengeti Ecosystem

THE GRASSLANDS OF THE SERENGETI and the Masai Mara must rank as one of the natural wonders of the world. There is the spectacle of the migration: a mass of millions of animals moving across the plains, crossing rivers dominated by

There are no fences on the border between the Serengeti and the Masai Mara. Animals such as this elephant move freely across the imaginary line on a map that took no account of ecological imperatives.

20-foot crocodiles and followed by predators waiting and watching for any opportunity. And it is fascinating that the timeless instinct of these animals to follow behind the rains is the key to the protection of the grasslands and their success.

Bernard Grzimek, director of the Frankfurt Zoological Gardens, and his son, Michael, who at the age of 23 was already an established documentary film producer, set off from Germany for Tanganyika in 1957. Their objective was to persuade the British government to rescind its decision to reduce the area of the Serengeti National Park by a third. They intended to carry out a scientific investigation of the annual migration that was to include an accurate count of the animals, a study of where they went, and analysis of the soil types and the grasses preferred by wildebeest, zebras, and gazelles. Alan Moorehead wrote the foreword to the Grzimeks' world-famous book *Serengeti Shall Not Die*. He noted their meticulous research and the precise grid they followed, which allowed every yard to be photographed and every head of game counted.

At the end of their studies the Grzimeks were able to conclude: "During several months of the year the new Serengeti Park will...contain no zebra and wildebeest and hardly any Thomson's gazelles. The 367,000 animals have to migrate across the borders to graze outside it, yet the whole object of creating the

ABOVE: *The dress of the Masai women at the village near Cottars 1920s Safari Camp reflects their rich culture.* RIGHT: *The Masai warrior, one of Africa's great conservationists, lives in harmony with nature.*

Serengeti National Park was so that the last remaining great herds of grassland animals in Africa should be protected within its borders all the year round." Bernard Grzimek continued, "The remaining portion of the Park will not be sufficient to maintain the existing herds."

Nonetheless, the British colonial government went ahead and excised the eastern portion of the plains and the famous Ngorongoro Crater from the Serengeti National Park. It was made into the Ngorongoro Conservation Area, in which it was planned that the Masai and their cattle would continue to live in harmony with wildlife. Contrary to the Grzimeks' fears, however, no fence was erected between the Serengeti and the Ngorongoro Conservation Area. This open-area philosophy was years ahead of its time and was the forerunner to the "biosphere reserve" concept, in which man and wildlife coexist.

A few years ago Dave Varty visited Tanzania with Valli Moosa, South Africa's minister for environmental affairs and tourism. They witnessed firsthand the benefits of not fencing, and Dave remembers, "we saw the need for mobility and

space for wild animals. In South Africa our wilderness areas are too often divided by fences that are not only unnecessary but are a hindrance to successful wildlife management." This principle was the basis for the formation of the transfrontier parks, which were instigated by the Peace Parks Foundation in South Africa.

Cottar's Kenya

In July 2002, when I visited Kenya at the start of the migration season, the Masai Mara was once again covered with a blanket of tall grass. As I stood on the imaginary line that marked the border between Kenya and Tanzania, the first herd of wildebeest appeared like a long black caravan from the well-cropped plains of the Serengeti. With them were zebras, Thomson's and Grant's gazelles, eland, buffalo, impalas, and hartebeest. About two million animals migrate into the Mara each year, crossing the crocodile-infested waters of the Mara and Grumeti Rivers to feed on the lush pastures swelled by the long rains of the previous months. After "wintering" and mating in the Mara, the migration returns south to the Serengeti, where, in an astonishing spectacle, hundreds of thousands of births take place in just a few weeks. By this time, due to the short rains of October and November, the grass of the Serengeti has recovered and is able to supply vital nutrients for the lactating mothers.

Since the 1950s, when the Grzimeks did their research, there has been a substantial increase in numbers, particularly of wildebeest. This was a result of the discovery in the 1960s of an inoculation against "yearling disease," to which both cattle and wildebeest were susceptible. The disease had appeared after the rinderpest epidemic just before the end of the 19th century and was thought to pass from antelope to cattle. But once the cattle were inoculated, the wildebeest started to thrive.

Charles Cottar arrived in East Africa soon after Theodore Roosevelt and was gripped by the spectacular panoramas and the challenge and excitement of this new frontier. The first American-born professional hunter in East Africa, he established Cottars Safari Service in 1919. The business has been handed down through four generations of the Cottar family, which continues to run photographic safari operations. Charles's grandson Glen and his wife, Pat, established the first tented camp for photographic safaris in Tsavo National Park in 1965.

Soon after hunting was banned in Kenya in 1977, Cottar's camp was built in a corner of the Masai Mara where Charles had often camped many years earlier. Today the Cottars 1920s Safari Camp is run by Glen and Pat's son, Calvin, and his wife, Louise. The tranquility of the Cottars' 100,000-acre exclusive wilderness on the Mara-Serengeti border is seldom disturbed by strangers—even if Calvin does not follow in his great-grandfather's footsteps by firing on any vehicle that comes into his territory. The camp, with its collection of memorabilia, immerses the visitor in the romance and drama of those early safari days. Here you will find the story of Charles's passion for Africa and for hunting that made him a legend in his own lifetime. *Continued on page 82*

Masai men and women wear jewelry made of multicolored beadwork.
The beadwork has a language, and each piece of jewelry tells its own story.

Wedding photo of Charles Cottar and Annette Bennett, 1897

Three generations of Cottars: Mona, Patricia Emily, Glen, Mike, Jean, and Charles

C HARLES AND ANNETTE COTTAR WERE CAPTIVATED BY THE TALES OF *Roosevelt's safari to Africa and wasted no time in leaving their Texas ranch, where Charles had earned his living in the saddle. He was a huge man, over six feet in height and with unusual physical strength. His dominating personality matched. So did his complete lack of fear. He became the first American professional hunter in East Africa. But he was both a hunter and a conservationist. When one group of clients wanted to shoot everything in sight, such was his disgust that he left them to fend for themselves.*

Syd Smith and party after a day's hunt

Mike Cottar takes aim from a motorbike, circa 1925

Charles Cottar and Mr. Phelps, Jr.

G. Phelps in camp with the spoils of an elephant hunt

Charles, after a close encounter

Three times Charles was mauled by leopards, which, he wrote depre-
catingly, "was enough." He was also gored by a buffalo and knocked
down by an elephant. Charles carried on undaunted until, while filming a charging rhino, he was mortally wounded. Only a year later, one
of his sons was killed by a buffalo. The legacy of Charles's love of Africa
and the business he founded, Cottars Safari Service, was carried on by
his son, his grandson, and now by Calvin Cottar, his great-grandson,
and his wife, Louise. The gist of their projects in the Mara is to ensure
that the local inhabitants receive a direct benefit from the wildlife on
their land.

Charles and his son Mike, after filming a lion kill in the Masai Mara, 1915

Continued from page 72

Today Calvin's major challenge is to involve the local Masai in conservation goals. Only a few decades ago the clans wandered with their cattle over the whole of the Mara, moving to green pastures wherever the sporadic rain fell. Then government programs created exclusive ranches for some Masai clans in an attempt to make the pastoralists more sedentary. Over time, the scheme backfired. Because rainfall was never predictable from year to year, the Masai overstocked their ranches as insurance against bad years when little rain fell. The overgrazing affected the food resources for wildlife, too, and an important lesson was learned.

Calvin works closely with his Masai landlords. A community of about 4,000 people benefit from his lease payments and the opportunities for training and employment at his camp, as well as assistance for education and health care. Apart from being a tenant, Calvin helps to build bridges of communication and understanding. "We need to prove to the Masai that a gerenuk could be worth a hundred head of cattle," says Calvin. "To make a breakthrough, we have to find a way of directly linking their economy to the wildlife. Wildlife laws need to change to allow landowners to own their wildlife and allow them to earn revenue from it any way they can. If we succeed, I believe that there could be a significant change in the Masai way of life."

Calvin believes the greatest danger to the future of wildlife in Kenya is the development program led by the government, which does not include wildlife. "They are legislating towards a land-use policy that is based on the premise that the 7.5 percent of Kenya's land allocated to game reserves is enough," he says. "This "island mentality" is setting up a further stage in the destruction of Kenya's biodiversity. With our climate, which includes long dry periods, islands of wildlife are not a sustainable solution. And when the government needs more land for agricultural development, they could look to areas like the Mara."

The Masai Mara National Reserve is one of Africa's most successful safari destinations. The Masai communities, who lease their land to safari operators such as Calvin, are increasingly becoming aware of the advantages of wildlife and are protecting wildlife against poaching. However, as in Ngorongoro, a major threat remains to the ecology of the region if the impact of tourism and human interference with natural systems are not monitored and controlled.

Ian Player, Magqubu Ntombela, and White Rhino

THE EASTERN SEABOARD OF SOUTH AFRICA, from the southern Mozambique border to the mouth of the St. Lucia Estuary, is a dramatic natural wilderness. Cyclones funnel

In 1908 Frederick Courteney Selous wrote: "The great square-mouthed rhinoceros…is now on the edge of extinction. I cannot think that the species will survive very far into the coming century." PRECEDING PAGES: *A blue wildebeest at sunrise in the 14,600-square-mile Kgalagadi Transfrontier Park*

down through the Mozambique Channel, and floods, droughts, heat, hail, and violent thunderstorms all have encores. The fickle climate on this coastal plain is matched by a rich variety of flora and fauna. The area of meandering rivers, chains of freshwater lakes, and saline estuaries was under the sea in recent geologic history. It is the only place in the world where hippos, crocodiles, and sharks share the same habitat. Nature went further to protect this paradise. For centuries an army of tsetse flies and mosquitoes kept farmers away from this beautiful but fragile land.

In 1890 it was estimated that there were 40 to 80 rhino left in the whole of southern Africa, and most of these were in the area proclaimed in 1897 as the Umfolozi Game Reserve. In 1919, after World War I, farmers moved into the area, and their conflict with wildlife and conservationists began. This conflict culminated during World War II, when nearly 140,000 animals were killed in and around the Umfolozi-Hluhluwe Reserves and farther north in Maputaland. After the war the wildlife had been decimated outside the reserves, but some animals within the reserves, including black and white rhinos, had survived and were flourishing.

When Ian Player joined the Natal Parks Board in 1952, the only park not under threat of deproclamation was Hluhluwe Game Reserve. Ian says, "All the rest of the reserves—Umfolozi, Mkuze, Ndumu, and St. Lucia—were under threat, either for resettlement, reforestation with exotic trees, or for cattle ranches. There was even talk about planting seed potatoes! That's how bad it was." He remembers the years of conflict that raged between farmers and wildlife, when farmers regarded the pristine land as perfect for crops and cattle. But even the most successful farmer, Oscar Curry, after 26 years—between 1919 and 1945—of trying to wrest a living from the land, gave up the fight against nature.

Over the years Ian Player learned much from his Zulu friend and mentor Magqubu Ntombela—not just of the ways of the wilderness but also of man's role in nature. Magqubu had a vast store of knowledge, passed down from generation to generation. He taught Ian that it was possible for humans and wildlife to live side by side, something that many conservationists thought impossible. It was all a matter of hard work, Magqubu told Ian. For example, picking the berries from a castor-oil bush, crushing them, and spreading them around a field would deter wild pigs from raiding his crops. He had an antidote for almost anything.

In 1953 Ian Player had counted 437 white rhinos in the Umfolozi Reserve—an area of about 72,000 acres. "Our problem," says Ian, "was that we had too many rhinos and not enough land. It was then that I, along with my colleagues, began one of the biggest battles of my life, lobbying politicians and anybody who would listen to get more land for wildlife. We were eventually successful, because today Umfolozi and Hluhluwe are joined together and the combined area under wildlife has increased to 275 square miles."

Alan Paton, who wrote the foreword to Ian Player's book, *The White Rhino Saga*, commented on Ian's next challenges: First, to repopulate the game reserves where white rhinos had once lived. Second, to supply white rhinos to the zoos of the world. Ian Player was so successful in achieving these goals that in the space of a decade, between January 1961 and March 1972, 1,109 white rhinoceros had been relocated. As early as 1965 IUCN (World Conservation Union) declared that the white rhino had been saved from extinction. Many had been moved to other reserves in Zululand and Maputaland, to the Kruger Park (where the last white rhino had been shot in 1896), and to Botswana, Mozambique, Zambia, and Zimbabwe. Some were sent as far afield as the Bronx and San Diego Zoos.

TOP ROW: *Blue wildebeest, Kudu* CENTER ROW: *Duiker, Gerenuk*
BOTTOM ROW: *Impala, Sable antelope*

They were even put back on the hunting list—a sure acceptance that the animal was safe. From 437 rhinoceros in the Umfolozi Game Reserve in 1953, the world population of white rhinoceros has increased to more than 12,000.

Many people behind the scenes had made the relocation of rhinos possible. Toni Harthoorn, a British scientist, developed the M99 capture drug in 1963; an American, Red Palmer, invented the Capchur gun, which could fire a loaded dart. And a dedicated team working under Col. Jack Vincent included Ian Player, Nick Steele, John Clarke, Owen Letley, and Magqubu Ntombela.

Before M99, capture operations were difficult and dangerous. Even big mammals were chased and lassoed from moving vehicles. The M99 capture drug made

As a result of the groundwork begun by Ian Player and Magqubu Ntombela under Natal Parks director Col. Jack Vincent, nearly 4,000 white rhinos and hundreds of black rhinos have been translocated—some dispersed around the globe—creating numerous gene pools and saving the two species from extinction.

capture operations much more efficient and brought other advantages to conservation. It became possible to sedate injured animals and treat wounds often made by poachers' snares. As a result of Ian's work, South Africa has become a leader in the industry of live relocations. Moving elephants has been particularly important because of their role in maintaining ecological balance and attracting tourists. They have been the key to unlocking the tourism potential of areas placed under conservation where farming has failed.

Ian went on to found the Wilderness Leadership School, an enlightened conservation tool. As Laurens van der Post wrote in the foreword to one of his many books, Ian Player's experience and his vision became "a compass for thousands seeking a trail of their own through the wilderness and wasteland of our time." Ian Player says, "It is the spiritual impact of the wilderness that will lead us to the higher ideals of conservation. It is this fact that has sustained me all my life." His farsighted philosophy was years ahead of the global consciousness that is becoming a trend in the 21st century.

The Vartys' Londolozi

THE BEGINNING OF THE LONDOLOZI STORY GOES BACK almost a hundred years to when James Stevenson-Hamilton began the recovery of South Africa's wildlife. It took a quarter century to have the Kruger National Park proclaimed, and with little

Soon after the spring rains, wildebeest are born in great numbers. The most wondrous spectacle of all is the birthing of wildebeest in southern Tanzania, when the great herds return from the annual migration.

funding available, Stevenson-Hamilton made compromises, one of which was to redraw the western border by swapping privately owned land under cattle within the park for land on the perimeter. A few months after the park was proclaimed in 1926, platinum was discovered in South Africa. TCL, the company that owned the land, decided that platinum mining would be preferable to cattle ranching in lion country, so it put its land up for sale. Two adventurers, Charles Varty and Frank Unger, heard the news while enjoying an afternoon of tennis in Johannesburg and bought the property sight unseen. This wilderness became their retreat and their love. For decades, little changed. Few visitors were prepared to risk the formidable journey by ox wagon over almost impassable tracks to get there.

John Varty, Charles's grandson, was seven months old when he went on his first safari, and shot a lion when he was 12. When his father died in 1969 he was 18, and he and his younger brother, Dave, became custodians of Sparta, as the ranch was then known. The two brothers had many problems to face on the farm that John renamed Londolozi—*the protector of all living things.* The wildlife that had been so abundant had all but disappeared, and, for the first time in living memory, the river that brought life to their corner of the bushveld stopped flowing. With little understanding of the obstacles that entrenched views could present, the young men surrounded themselves with like-minded young people. So began the Londolozi experience. Essential to the conservation model that evolved were land restoration, the reintroduction of animals, and the creation of tourist accommodations. However, the key to their success was engaging the skills and support of local communities and ensuring a two-way flow of economic benefits.

The metamorphosis of Londolozi began with the Varty brothers' determination to solve the riddle of why certain species were disappearing while others were on the increase. Lions were so scarce that visitors were taken out in their pajamas at midnight if a roar was heard. At first no one they approached was able to give satisfactory answers to their questions; then John and Dave met an ecologist named Ken Tinley. He was able to interpret the landscape, and he taught John and Dave how it fitted together. "The problem had started with overgrazing of the grasslands by cattle," says Dave. "Our grandparents and their friends naturally selected a route through open grasslands, which would have been dry in winter. Their ox wagons, the American-style buckboard, and later their cars traveled over the same areas where cattle had grazed and where zebra and wildebeest concentrated in winter. The result was that the soils on the hillsides compacted, forming a barrier to water. Instead of rainwater seeping into the soils, it ran off, faster and faster as the gullies eroded, and the land slowly dried out.

"This drying-out process was exacerbated by further concentrations of game after the Kruger Park erected a fence on our eastern boundary," Dave continues. "Although it was put up in the name of veterinary protection, it took no account of geo-ecological features such as river systems, and it restricted the movement of animals, with disastrous results."

John and Dave, who were then ten and seven, were to see the immediate effects of this fence, which was dubbed "the Berlin Wall of Conservation." Dave says: "We were out with warden Harry Kirkman patrolling the fence one day when we saw about 450 buffalo on the Kruger side of the fence, all with their noses toward the Sand River, which was inaccessible to them. Harry cut the barbed wire and chased the buffalo into the Sabi Sand, repairing the fence behind him. That's how we got our buffalo. Even worse was the plight of the wildebeest that were stopped at the fence from reaching the river and their winter grazing. The western wildebeest population crashed from 25,000 to 752 and 40 years later has still not recovered.

"At the time," he continues, "most people thought Ken Tinley's approach was too radical, but he was the first to recognize the connection between the drying-out process and scrub encroachment. His recommendation was clear and simple: 'Clear the bush in the lower valleys and use the branches to plug the

Continued on page 96

Winnis Mathebula and Boyd Varty with lion kill

Friends load up the buckboard.

"**N**OTHING COULD HAVE PREPARED CHARLES VARTY AND FRANK *Unger for the beauty of the bushveld estate they had bought,"* says Dave Varty, grandson of Charles. *"Trekking on foot toward the Sand River in 1926, they would have caught glimpses of roan and sable antelope, waterbuck, and herds of wildebeest, and perhaps heard the distant roar of a lion. It was the start of a love affair that has endured through four generations of Varty and Unger families, including my father, Boyd, and Betty Taylor, whose son, Allan, is our partner at Londolozi."*

Shan Watson in the outdoor "shower"

The Ford makes its way over the Sabi Sand.

Members of the Varty and Unger families after hunting a lion on foot

Charles Varty with daughter Nan and friends

Hunter-naturalist Two-tone Sithole

Dave, age 9, steadies rifle on Boyd's shoulder.

Betty Taylor, Frank Unger's daughter

"The hunting ethics practiced by my grandfather and my father and our guide, Winnis Mathebula, were instilled in me and my brother as children. We learnt how to handle a gun, to go out at first light and only on foot, with no vehicles and no telescopic sights. We were taught to listen to the sounds of the wild, to glean information from the bush telegraph system—the warning calls from the birds and the distress signals of the antelope—and how to follow fresh lion tracks in the morning dew.

"For both of us, the switch from hunter to conservationist was a natural extension of our bushveld life. In a way, our hunting techniques paved the way for photographic safaris, but we were directed there by our growing awareness that the game was disappearing and that something had to be done about it."

The mud hut rondavels that replaced the founders' tents on the banks of the Sand River

Continued from page 89

eroded gullies that carry away the precious rain. Restore the high water table. The grass will grow, and the animals will return.' He also recognized, years ahead of his time, the need to connect disadvantaged communities to the economic benefits of the wilderness."

While John devoted himself to the task of land rehabilitation, Dave and Shan looked after the lodges and the visitors. "For every rand we earned in tourism, we spent 1.2 rand on the land, and we lived in overdraft," recalls Dave. "Sometimes, when the bank manager arrived at Londolozi, we would be forewarned and would slink out the back and be gone 'into the bush for the day.' It was an endless tug of war. We worked beyond ourselves for two decades. I believe that is why Londolozi is such an unbelievable paradise of animals and birds today. We discovered that if you work with nature, her bounty is never-ending."

Fortunately, Dave and John had found Ken Tinley in time to rebuild the micro-catchment areas of Londolozi and repair the erosion caused by cattle tracks and roads that turned into rivers of mud in the wet season. Coincidentally, the first sightings of a mother leopard began with the clearing program. John Varty, together with his great friend and colleague Elmon Mhlongo, spent several years tracking this wonderful leopard. One year they lived a completely nocturnal existence, following her night after night through the thick bush. They filmed her life, watching her groom her cubs, hunt, and fight for her territory with another leopard and eventually seeing her attacked and mortally wounded by lions. Altogether she brought nine sets of cubs into the world and started a dynasty that provides guests with unforgettable wildlife experiences. Once rarely sighted, there are now 30 of these unpredictable and stunningly beautiful cats under observation at Londolozi. Recently two females and four cubs were seen together—an extraordinary sighting.

Today, many people from the local community operate small businesses that supply Londolozi with products and services, while Londolozi employs men and women as rangers and trackers, cameramen, managers, teachers, nurses, chefs, mechanics, waiters, and cleaners. Londolozi is all about giving people opportunity and hope. Whether it was for children's education, health, jobs, business opportunity, or equity involvement, care of people was the third leg of Londolozi's three-legged model: care of land, care of wildlife, and care of people.

Londolozi Game Reserve is renowned for its leopard sightings. FOLLOWING PAGES: *Wildebeest and zebras take a chance swimming the Mara River on their way to the rich grasslands of the Masai Mara. It could mean a fatal meeting with a 20-foot-long Nile crocodile.*

Chapter Four

The Pathfinders

B Y THE END OF THE 1980S SOUTH AFRICA CARED AS LITTLE TO LOOK BACK
as it did to look forward. The chasm between the past and the future was
enormous, but out of the chaos of the dying days of apartheid one man emerged to
give all South Africans hope—Nelson Mandela. He had a rare combination of
qualities: intelligence, compassion, understanding, a willingness to listen, and the
generosity to forgive those who had jailed him for nearly 30 years. Over the previous decade, when sanctions against South Africa had bitten deep, tourism had a
tough time trying to survive. Government-owned national parks and reserves were
heavily subsidized, and it was widely expected that the new government would place

ABOVE: *Toxic seeds of the rosary pea* OPPOSITE: *Giraffes bend and stretch their long
graceful necks.* PRECEDING PAGES: *A lioness relocated to the Phinda Game Reserve checks on her cubs.*

wildlife low on their list of priorities. The investment climate for tourism and conservation was poor. However, in February 1990 Nelson Mandela was released, and anticipation of South Africa's reentry onto the world stage triggered a reemergence of the safari industry in South Africa.

Six months earlier, in July 1989, Richard Leakey's pyre of ivory was a turning point. Leakey, with President Moi's support, gave notice of his determination to put an end to the corruption and poaching that had seen the destruction of 90 percent of the elephant and rhino populations and much other wildlife. Kenya, in its heyday, was magnificent. Its natural wealth should have been the foundation of an independent future. Instead, the growth of tourism, explosive in the 1970s, lost impetus. The relentless rise in population and agriculture and a consequent destruction of habitat, as well as—despite all Leakey's efforts—continued poaching, did not bode well for the long-term future of Kenya's wildlife.

One difference between South Africa and Kenya was that about 30 years ago South Africa adopted legislation passing ownership of wildlife to landowners. The disadvantage was that the new law encouraged the fencing in of moveable property, and no one wanted to watch a black rhino worth $50,000 walk off onto a neighboring farm. You could even get tax deductions on the fences you built. The advantage was that commercial utilization of wildlife grew by leaps and bounds to the extent that two-thirds of the 90,000 square miles under wildlife in South Africa is owned by the private sector and used for tourism, hunting and shooting, game ranching, and commercial sales of live animals and venison.

In Kenya and elsewhere on the continent ownership of wildlife is still vested in the government, with the result that the population has little interest in conserving wildlife because of the perception that it has no value to them. This viewpoint is particularly pertinent for the Masai, Ndorobo, and Samburu tribal areas, where pastoral nomadism still prevails as a way of life. Because these areas are mostly semiarid and will support neither agriculture nor any significant increase in pastoral farming, there is a fundamental need to change attitudes and beliefs about the value of wildlife. It is out of this need that a new generation of conservationists has emerged in East Africa, one that believes that conservation goals cannot be achieved without cooperation and support of local communities.

The reemergence of South Africa's Garden of Eden
IN SOUTH AFRICA, APART FROM THE KRUGER PARK, there were no vast areas set aside for wildlife. For the most part reserves were relatively small islands amid a sea of

The Drakensberg sugarbush (Protea dracomontana) *is found on the escarpment that runs parallel to the Indian Ocean through KwaZulu-Natal and Mpumalanga, where the mountains overlook the big-game country of the Kruger National Park.*

rural villages and unsustainable agricultural development. To create an eco-tourism industry, it was essential to find ways to advance green frontiers, take down fences, and, where possible, link these small islands of wilderness together.

The first task was to identify assets that were underperforming or dormant, largely as a result of the political ideologies of apartheid, and resuscitate them. The "assets" consisted mainly of vacant or neglected land, private and government owned, where farming had been tried and had failed. There was vacant land in the Karoo, where, at the height of the wool industry, 40 million sheep had grazed. Left behind were silted dams, erosion, rivers so overused that they stopped flowing in dry seasons, and vegetation devastated by nearly 200 years of unsustainable farming. An eerie silence enveloped these areas. There were also large tracts of land in the Eastern Cape near the Addo Elephant National Park, inland from Port Elizabeth and Algoa Bay, where sheep and cattle farming had proved unprofitable. Two hours north of Johannesburg was another vast unutilized wilderness—the Waterberg. Yet another area with potential was the coastal zone south of Mozambique, where many people had been relocated during the apartheid era. This land—with its thin crust of poor soils—included

the Greater St. Lucia Wetland Park, recognized as a World Heritage site in 1999. Even the vast area covered by the Kruger National Park was an under-performing asset.

Here was an opportunity for private conservancy programs and rural communities to participate by converting land unsuitable for agriculture to wildlife. But restoring land and relocating wildlife were easier said than done. First there was no money, then there were laws against moving wild animals, objections to having dangerous game—or wildlife that might carry disease—close to farms, and, possibly the most difficult of all, entrenched prejudice within the government-owned and government-managed reserves against any private enterprise venture

LEFT: *Dolphins chase the annual sardine migration up the coast of KwaZulu-Natal and into the Maputaland Marine Reserve.* ABOVE: *Female ostrich*

that might compete with their virtual monopoly of the wildlife business.

On the other hand, South Africa had some real advantages: the technology to relocate wildlife and experience in repairing damaged ecosystems. On the horizon was a new government with an open mind. It was against this background that the first significant eco-tourism project by private enterprise in South Africa emerged. Conservation Corporation aimed to bring business discipline and international investment to conservation. In 1989 the corporation identified a 60-square-mile parcel of land that linked two government-owned Maputaland reserves and created the opportunity for community partnerships. To the west was the Mkuze Game Reserve, one of the few places in Africa with both black and white rhinos. To the east lay the St. Lucia Estuary, and beyond it a unique combination of habitats including coastal dune forests, mangrove and palm forests, golden beaches, and a marine reserve stretching offshore to coral reefs that supported a great variety of aquatic life. It was a paradise for mammals, birds, and reptiles, including leatherback and loggerhead turtles, frogs, butterflies, and countless insect species.

CCAfrica—as the corporation came to be known—considered Maputaland one of the most significant remaining wilderness areas in Africa. Yet only a few years earlier there had been a major conflict—this time between the conservationists and those who wanted to strip the coast of its sands to recover heavy minerals such as titanium, rutile, and zircon. The KwaZulu-Natal Parks Board won, and when the noise died down it was up to the conservationists to develop the area with the least impact on the land.

CCAfrica believed that their project, which they called Phinda, meaning "The Return," could show the way. Their challenge was to prove that wildlife could outperform cattle and agriculture and stimulate a regional economy that was lifeless. Those were the dynamics around which Phinda was built. Dave Varty, one of the founders of CCAfrica, says: "There was no understanding or belief that you could take derelict agricultural farms and convert them to wildlife as an investment. When I went to New York it was pioneering work for the investors. What I was asking for was a significant leap of faith." His first attempt in New York went something like this: "We are aware that Nelson Mandela is calling for sanctions against South Africa. And our game reserve is situated right in the middle of a potential civil war between the Zulu leader Mangosuthu Buthelezi and Mandela's ANC. And there are none of the Big Five—elephant, rhino, lion, leopard, buffalo—that attract tourists, and we have a lot of work to do to get rid of rusty farm equipment, broken fences, and dense bush that has invaded neglected farmlands. But I believe that Phinda will turn out to be a better investment than gold!" Needless to say, the portfolio manager was not convinced.

Phinda Game Reserve succeeded and it endures. It has created jobs, has become a catalyst for change in the rural economy, and is a spectacular safari destination. Although many animals had been relocated, there were few to be seen at first. The relocated herd of young elephants hid in the forest whenever they heard a Land Rover approach. Leopards continued to be wary of humans. It would be several years before the bush-clearing program would make any impact and lions and cheetahs could be seen. More often than not Phinda's rangers had little choice but to entertain their guests by discussing the finer details of the sex life of a frog or a wasp. Phinda's success revolved around a team of people who brought very different personal contributions. Mark Getty and

TOP ROW: *Pencilled surgeonfish, Honeycomb moray eel* CENTER ROW: *Crescent-tail big-eye, Coachman* BOTTOM ROW: *Coral rockcod, Semicircle angel fish* FOLLOWING PAGES: *A coming of age is celebrated with dancing in the green hills of KwaZulu-Natal.*

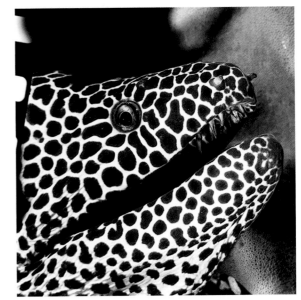

his family foundation provided financial stability and confidence, Les Carlisle brought the practical hard work necessary to make a difference in the field, and Dave Varty introduced the Londolozi model, which directed Phinda toward involving local communities as well as using sustainable conservation practices.

One of their first jobs was to call a meeting with the local community leaders and tell them what they planned to do: how they would bring back the lions and the elephants (and the dangers that were involved), and how they would compensate their neighbors if a lion took any of their cattle. Dave also spoke about providing jobs and training for their neighbors and about a fund they would set up to help with education and health. Simon Gumede, a member of the KwaZulu parliament and the leader of the Mduku community on their eastern boundary, was skeptical. He was a wise man who wondered if these young men had any idea how hard their job would be.

It took a decade to put things right. Today Phinda is a tribute to its founders, who endured hardships to create an exemplary conservation model. It is a stunning example of what humans can do to repair the land and give nature a helping hand in reestablishing lost species. It is also an example of what can be achieved in symbiotic relationships. Phinda, with the help of its safari guests, has been able to set up a clinic, build classrooms and provide computers, establish scholarship programs, and help small-business development.

The next logical step will be the development of community-owned ecotourism projects. Phinda staff member Gladys Zikhali believes that Phinda is a role model in helping everyone to unite within the environmental equation. The Rural Investment Fund, started at Phinda and developed into the Africa Foundation, is helping rural people to participate wherever a lodge is prepared to participate and manage the program. Just recently Isaac Tembe, who started at Phinda as a community liaison officer, has been appointed to the Africa Foundation board.

Phinda has also been able to reduce poaching significantly. "We were well aware when we started Phinda," says Les Carlisle, a member of CCAfrica's conservation committee, "that you cannot expect to remain an island of wealth amid a sea of poverty. We involved our rural neighbors and reconnected them to the land. They do not want to see poachers from Mozambique taking 'their' animals. The result is that over a period of a decade we have drastically reduced the number of snares found on our property."

No two zebras have exactly the same markings. The stripes of Burchell's zebras can be broad or narrow, and the shadow stripes can be distinct or even absent. FOLLOWING PAGES: *Tree agama, or lizard, at Phinda Game Reserve*

At the 2002 Earth Summit, Phinda was recognized for its achievements. The reserve won one category—Best Contribution to the Natural Environment—in the Imvelo Responsible Tourism Awards. It was also a finalist in two more categories, and came out the overall winner. Phinda has stimulated a regional economy that was dead. The road that was moved has given rural people access to markets—which have expanded significantly. "Phinda has altered many people's attitudes," says Les Carlisle. "Ten years ago we were told we would never be able to move the road on our west boundary—between us and Mkuze Game Reserve. We did. Then we were told that the fences between us and the state reserves would never come down and that privately owned land would never form part of the Greater St. Lucia Wetland World Heritage Site. That too is in process."

Phinda has been a catalyst for the proliferation of land-restoration projects and has proved that derelict farmland can be converted to wildlife. Not only have land values increased, the escalation in the value of wildlife—on land intended for wildlife—has been spectacular. "We started at Phinda with 15 cheetah," says Les Carlisle. "Predator reintroductions in the past had not been successful. Currently Phinda has 25 cheetah. We've sold 45 and we know that 25 have escaped—into our neighboring reserves. The lions have not been quite as successful because they are susceptible to snares. If an antelope gets caught in a snare, the lions will run in and investigate. As most snare lines are laid with eight to ten snares, lions often get caught."

Phinda has been a pathfinder for conservation. Les Carlisle says: "The Londolozi model became a South African model and the vehicle for launching a new industry. It set benchmarks that involved rural communities. This was the key to our success. If we don't support the local economies outside the parks, we will lose our wilderness islands. This is what got Dave Varty motivated at Londolozi. It hasn't changed. It took CCAfrica into the first partnership with National Parks with the development of Ngala—the first private enterprise project within the Kruger Park. It took us up into East Africa, into Kenya and Tanzania."

Kenya and Lewa Downs

SOUTH AFRICA HAD BEEN THE FIRST COUNTRY IN AFRICA south of the Sahara to stand by and watch its wildlife devastated. It was appropriate that it was also the first on the comeback trail. Others were to follow. In the 1960s it seemed impossible that Kenya's abundant wildlife could be endangered, but it was. Once again there were people who were prepared to do something about it.

Lewa Downs, on the rolling hills to the north of Mount Kenya, lies on the ancient migration route that elephants had taken for thousands of years—until the second half of the 20th century: from the well-watered slopes of Mount Kenya north through Lewa to the dry bush country that is now Marsabit National Park and the Northern Frontier District of Kenya.

Soon after independence in 1963, the government bought the Craig family farm in the highlands between the Great Rift Valley and Lake Victoria for resettlement. The family moved their entire farming operation to marginal land at Lewa Downs, where their forebears had first settled in 1922. When Ian and Will Craig took over from their father in 1977 they decided to downscale cattle farming and reintroduce wildlife. They could not have started at a worse time. That year hunting was banned in Kenya, and a decade of unprecedented poaching got under way. The black rhino population of Kenya fell from 20,000 to a few hundred. White rhinos and elephants were systematically slaughtered, and the beautiful Grevy's zebra found on Lewa Downs faced extinction.

The turning points in the fortunes of Lewa Downs came first in 1983, with the start of a sanctuary for black rhinoceros, and then in 1988, when poachers slaughtered a herd of elephants. Ian realized that unless the Masai were involved directly in conservation, the wildlife was doomed—and with the animals gone the land would be damaged by overpopulations of cattle. This was the background against which Ian and Will Craig formed the Lewa Wildlife Conservancy (LWC) in 1993. Ian had set in motion a project that would send ripples outward and bring new people and land under a conservation ethic. It had started with a core area of 40,000 acres. Then the Ngare Ndare National Forest Reserve was fenced into the conservancy, increasing the area under conservation by another 16,000 acres.

Today, Ian Craig's blue eyes sparkle with enthusiasm when he talks about the Masai community-owned and community-hosted eco-lodges he has helped establish: the Sarara tented camp, owned by the Namunyak community, and Il N'gwesi Lodge on Lewa's northern border. These first two lodges are acting as a catalyst, and already a third Masai project, Tassia Lodge at Lekurruki, is up and running. With the support of LWC, the Masai owners have learned far more than how to provide guests with exciting wildlife experiences. They have learned how to maintain their traditional agricultural and pastoral way of life in harmony with wildlife and how to protect water catchments and thereby the integrity of the land. The Masai communities also act

as a buffer between Lewa and the poachers, and the extended wildlife area has given elephants greater freedom to roam.

Recently at the World Summit on Sustainable Development, Il N'gwesi—out of 400 entries—was one of seven winners of the Equator Prize 2000. The Masai Il N'gwesi community was able to show the positive impact they have made. Socially they have broken with tradition by sending young girls to school. They have recovered flora on land damaged by overgrazing. Wildlife has returned and poaching has been more or less eliminated and, through the introduction of tourism, they have the foundations for a sustainable economic business. Ian had hoped that within a decade Lewa Downs and the Masai lodges would be self-sufficient. However, the fragility of

At 17,058 feet, the snow-crowned peak of Mount Kenya towers above the 276-square-mile Mount Kenya National Park. The local Kikuyu people call the mountain Kirinyaga, "mountain of whiteness," and regard it as the sacred home of Ngai, their god.

the international tourism industry is proving to be a difficult challenge and is forcing Lewa to look for alternative sustainable funding mechanisms.

The task for LWC has not been easy, as Ian's plans have always stretched far beyond Lewa's budget. The straight facts are that without donor funding Lewa cannot balance its budget. "We could if we stayed within our boundaries," comments Ian. "But our ambition for the future is to involve all the Masai communities of the district in conservation." Part of Ian's year is spent fund-raising in Europe and America. He has many good friends, particularly Iain Douglas Hamilton of Save the Elephant, the UK-based charity Tusk Trust, and WWF—the World Wide Fund for Nature. Just one of Ian's many fund-raising projects is a unique high-altitude marathon run on Lewa Downs that attracts runners from all over the world.

Lewa, with Mount Kenya dominating the landscape on a clear day, is a magical place. Since Ian and Will took over, Grevy's zebras have flourished and Lewa Downs has become an exporter, not only of zebras but also of reticulated giraffes and white rhinos, which have done well since their introduction. Today Lewa has an equal number of white and black rhinos—32 of each. With Lewa's perfect habitat for *sitatunga*, Richard Leakey suggested to Ian that they might like to introduce these secretive aquatic antelopes. Can you imagine catching sitatunga? You can't reach them by vehicle in the swamps. You can't

Visitors to Lewa Downs are captivated by the variety of bird life: Red-billed buffalo weavers, hoopoes, rollers, kingfishers, starlings, barbets, and this Jackson's hornbill, which poses on the veranda railing. FOLLOWING PAGES: *Two female leopards engage in a ferocious territorial dispute.*

dart them because they may drown before you get to them. The solution that Ian's team came up with was to physically jump on them, straight out of a helicopter. They relocated the first sitatunga from Lake Victoria, near Kisumu, where a decade ago they were able to see 10 to 15 in their watery habitat every day. "We've been back there recently," says Ian, "but have not seen a single animal on the three trips we made over the same swamps. We can only assume that they are extinct there." In the meantime the original ten sitatunga relocated to Lewa have increased more than fivefold.

To ensure the increase in wildlife at Lewa, Ian has kept predator species low and his security force high; the latter accounts for one-third of Lewa's budget. There is only one pride of lions on the farm, and one of the females is collared so staff are always aware of the pride's location. That does not detract from the natural wildness of the land and is very much in line with the history of the Kruger National Park in South Africa, where Stevenson-Hamilton had lions shot to restore the prey herds. Ian does not go as far as shooting lions, however. There are many places in Kenya where they can be relocated.

Perhaps the most ambitious of all Ian's plans is to link together wilderness areas and reinstate the migration route of the elephants—all the way from the 250,000-square-mile arid Northern Frontier District to Mount Kenya National Park. Looking at a plan on a map is nothing like looking at reality. Even creating a narrow corridor of land into the park will be a formidable undertaking. As would be expected in a country with little prime agricultural land, the lower slopes of Mount Kenya are intensely cultivated. Creating a corridor through this maze of farms will not be easy. A recent report by Bongo Woodley, senior warden of the 276-square-mile Mount Kenya National Park, contains an indication of the problems facing Ian. Within the Mount Kenya reserve he found 14,600 trees individually cut down, an additional 19,760 acres of indigenous forest clear-cut, 2,400 charcoal kilns, thousands of cattle, sheep, and goats, 500 acres of marijuana, and lots of small agricultural plots. Like the Grzimeks he pilots a small aircraft to find out what is happening on the land. But on the slopes of Mount Kenya, it's no easy task. When teased about flying only a hundred feet above the treetops, he gave a wry smile and replied: "At that height you catch too many downdrafts. It's better to fly lower!"

When Ian started working with the Masai he realized that he would have to earn their trust. He did this in several ways. Lewa became an engine for economic growth—finding capital for new developments, relocating animals, and assisting with health care, water supply, education, and security. Five schools attached to the Lewa Conservancy have been established, and scholarships for 24 young men and women to further their studies are provided. Will and his wife, Emma, who have continued to run the farm and the safari business outside the conservancy, have started industries employing local craftspeople. Both the Kifuma carpet workshop, which uses Ethiopian weaving techniques, and the furniture workshop are hives of activity. Will is also working on a project to replant forests of acacia well liked by impalas and elephants.

What Ian and Will's efforts add up to is a wedge that could shift a great weight of opinion in Kenya. Poaching has not stopped. Lewa reported that ten rhinos were poached in the last two weeks of October 2002, and there has been a noticeable increase in elephant poaching. Nonetheless, a trend has been set, and Ian believes there are some good years ahead for wildlife: "The community projects are catching," he says, "and the more money they make the more contagious they will be." It is a bright ray of hope for the future of the wildlife and the beautiful wilderness of Kenya.

Chapter Five

A Jewel in
the Wilderness

TAKING UP A CAMERA INSTEAD OF A GUN CHANGED MANY ASPECTS OF THE
safari. It brought the thrill and adventure of driving or walking in the
bush to a much wider audience. Dave Varty says: "The years we had spent hunting
had taught us a lot about animal behavior. We knew how to track lions and how to
get up close. We knew about alarm calls and about the reactions of prey species. In
the early years of photography we used our hunting/tracking technique to find
exciting big game. When we put down our guns we started another journey and
learnt so much more about nature and the spirit that flows from the wilderness.

ABOVE: *Warthog tusk* OPPOSITE: *Standing over its impala kill, a cheetah pauses to recover its breath
after the chase.* PRECEDING PAGES: *Blue wildebeest walk away from a water hole in the Savuti Marsh.*

"People on safari became far more interested in learning about the whole food chain, from insects and birds upwards," continues Dave. They wanted to know about the family relationships of animals and how they react to one another and their neighbors. They wanted to know about landscape patterns and ecosystems, about different grasses and trees, about the geological features, such as how the peaks of Kilimanjaro were formed, why the Victoria Falls has changed its position in the riverbed through time, what has caused the rivers of the Okavango to change direction. People also wanted involvement with nature. New activities such as riding elephants through herds of animals, flying over the cataracts on the Zambezi

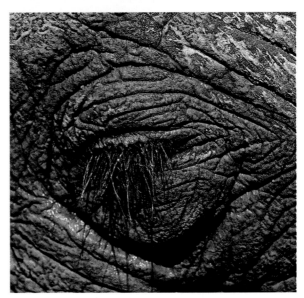

ABOVE: *An elephant's eye is protected from the sun by four-inch-long lashes.* LEFT: *The tawny golden eyes of a lioness, Africa's top predator*

below the Falls, climbing to the glaciers on Mount Kenya and Kilimanjaro, sitting in a forest with a gorilla family, swimming with dolphins or whale sharks all became popular. A new generation of birdwatchers became fascinated by the array of bird life that was so accessible.

A whole new industry was being born. The hunting safari had been for the privileged few. The photographic safari and the great outdoor African adventure—combined with the warm hospitality of Africa's people—gave the continent a chance to be globally competitive and to become the adventure destination of the world.

Before South Africa had embarked on its comeback trail, one country in southern Africa was already moving in a different direction from most of its neighbors. Overlooking a few hiccups here and there, the tourism industry in Botswana was on its way to becoming the second largest contributor to the country's national income. Today, only diamonds earn more.

Much of Botswana's success was a matter of timing. Early in the 20th century, when farmers from Europe were looking for more and more land in Africa, Botswana was well protected by the tsetse fly and the mosquito. Nobody wanted any part of it. At that stage the beauty of the Okavango was largely untouched. The country's prime minister, Sir Seretse Khama, had little trouble gaining independence for his country, which was listed among the 20 poorest in the world. Just over a year later, in 1967, Botswana was on its way to becoming the world's largest producer by value of diamonds. The result was that the wilderness areas of the country were pristine while at the same time Botswana had money—for education, for development of infrastructure, and most of all for helping to create jobs for its people.

Nearly 40 percent of Botswana's total surface area has been proclaimed as wildlife reserves or is under wildlife management—more than any other country in Africa with the exception of Tanzania. In northern Botswana, nearly half the economically active population is employed in the wildlife industry. Sir Seretse's son, Ian Khama, who started his career in the army and trained at Sandhurst, becoming head of the Botswana military and more recently vice president of Botswana, is largely responsible. Ian Khama's love of nature and his determination to stamp out poaching have resulted in a flourishing and sustainable industry. He was involved in establishing the Botswana model, which focuses on small private lodges and groups that seldom number more than 24 people—and more often fewer than 16—that make little impact on the pristine wilderness. In Botswana, the private sector has been allowed to take a lead in establishing tourism while the government supports and regulates the sector. This is somewhat unusual in Africa, where there is often too much government interference.

Colin Bell, CEO of Wilderness Safaris, says: "Forget big lodges. If you want to feel the heart and soul of Africa, you have to hear the footsteps of the buffalo, the songs of the birds, and the roar of the lion. You need privacy for that timeless magic to get under your skin." Twenty-five years ago, as a ranger, Colin spent nearly all his time in Botswana. He believed that the company he worked for should establish a base in Botswana. Despite his entreaties, his boss resisted making any change. So Colin took the plunge. He resigned, and he and his partner, Chris MacIntyre, started their own safari business based in Maun, initially running birding and camping safaris. Six years later Wilderness Safaris acquired Mombo, a virtually unknown camp on the edge of Chief's Island. With the help of tracker Joseph Tekenekso and a formidable pack of wild dogs, Mombo has become the star of the Wilderness Safaris group, which operates in five countries in Africa and the Seychelles. "Today," Colin says, "we manage 40 camps and have private access to about 4,000 square miles of southern Africa's finest wilderness. Nearly half our camps are in Botswana and Namibia."

The Okavango Delta is an emerald gem where the rivers from the mountains of Angola meander aimlessly over nearly 6,000 square miles of wilderness to form a delta on a sea of sand where they finally evaporate. Along the way streams feed waving beds of papyrus, hippo grass, and water lilies, and in turn they feed the hippopotamus, the buffalo and elephant, the lechwe and the sitatunga. Each year, as the floodwaters recede, fish are caught in pools that slowly dry out. It is then that the birds have a field day. Saddle-bill storks wade into the water looking for fish or frogs, which they jab with their long bills, African fish eagles watch from a nearby perch and then swoop in for fish. Pied kingfishers hover over the water and then turn, tail up, and dive, while the jewel-like malachite and pygmy kingfishers wait their turn in the reeds.

Colin believes that all nature-based tourism companies should be involved in conservation issues. He says: "With Africa's most effective antipoaching program in place, we are working with the Department of Wildlife on reintroducing rhinos into the Moremi Game Reserve." The first white rhinos are already here and many more are on their way as a result of an exchange program with South Africa's national parks: rhino for sable. Another project, dubbed Children in the Wilderness, got under way when Paul Newman visited Wilderness Safaris' camps in 2001. With Paul's support and the experience of his Hole in the Wall organization for helping terminally ill children, a program for disadvantaged children from villages on the fringes of the Okavango was set up. In January 2003, with Paul Newman's organization sending trainers and helping with funding, some 370 children in Botswana spent a week at various camps. The children were given opportunities to learn about their wildlife heritage and about local arts and crafts and to participate in writing classes and theater productions. Most of all, they had fun.

Wilderness Safaris is also involved with the Torra Wildlife Conservancy, which was set up with the local community in Namibia—a favorite country of Colin, of which he says: "There is something so very special about the endless vistas of the desert, the huge expanse of the sky, the mists that roll in from the icy Atlantic, and the various life-forms that scrape their tenuous existence from the desert." Other Wilderness Safaris conservation projects in southern Africa include an antipoaching program in Malawi, in conjunction with Frankfurt Zoological Society, and a wild dog research project in the Okavango.

FOLLOWING PAGES: *Lechwes take flight through the shallow waters of Botswana's Okavango Delta. Few predators will follow them through the watery wilderness.*

A JEWEL IN THE WILDERNESS

In the far north of Botswana Jonathan Gibson, co-owner of Chobe Game Lodge, remembers the early days on the Chobe River. "Just a few miles upstream from us is a derelict village, Serondela, that has quite a history. Originally the houses were for employees of a timber mill built to exploit the fine Rhodesian teak forests. Eventually all the timber near the mill had been chopped down and the mill became uneconomical. When the mill closed my father was one of a handful of people who bought one of the mill houses for our annual holidays from South Africa. That was where I grew to love the wilderness. For years after Chobe was proclaimed in 1968 we were allowed to stay, but eventually we were asked to leave the reserve. For a while, before the cattle herds were depleted by foot-and-mouth disease and tsetse fly, the abandoned houses were used by the Batswana on their way to the market at Livingstone. Today, a pride of lions has taken over one of the houses."

As well as owning the Chobe Game Lodge, which he bought in 1983, Jonathan, with Pat Carr-Hartley, created the Chobe Wildlife Trust with the objective of assisting the Department of Wildlife and National Parks with ecological and wildlife research and the reintroduction of species indigenous to the region. Jonathan has also taken a special interest in the Caprivi, on the opposite bank of the Chobe River. "At the notorious conference in Berlin that oversaw the division of the African continent in the late 1800s," he told us, "Germany was given jurisdiction over South-West Africa and German East Africa while the British sphere of influence included Northern and Southern Rhodesia. Soon afterward Germany negotiated with Britain for an exchange of land to create an east-west corridor between their two territories. In the end Germany took a stretch of land giving them access to the Zambezi that became known as the Caprivi [named after Leo von Caprivi, who headed up the negotiations] and Britain took over Zanzibar. In more recent times Botswana and Namibia have fought tooth and nail over a small piece of the Caprivi known as Kasikili-Sedudu Island, in the middle of the Chobe River. However, the World Court in The Hague has returned ownership of this island to Botswana.

"The problem we have with the Caprivi," says Jonathan, "is that the people there are predominantly pastoralists. They don't want wildlife—especially the lions that regularly swim across the Chobe to take a swipe at a tasty piece of beef. I decided that I would try to show them that there were other ways of making a living and built the Safari Lodge on the north bank of the Chobe. They have learned that they can earn

TOP ROW: *Leopard with cub, Elephants locked in a friendly greeting* CENTER ROW: *White rhino and calf, Giraffe mother and child* BOTTOM ROW: *Warthog family, Lioness and cubs*

In Serondela, a pride of lions has taken over a house once constructed for employees of a timber mill.
FOLLOWING PAGES: *An elephant is silhouetted against the fleeting African dawn in Chobe National Park.*

more working in the lodge, and it is a start—perhaps for them to build their own camps one day. The aim of the Caprivi Conservancy, which we are helping to set up with local NGOs, is to have more people benefit directly from the wilderness."

On a recent visit to Botswana I had the opportunity to listen to the Chobe elephants. It was not a song—it was a lament. We were watching a herd of elephants that were completely relaxed as they walked slowly away from the river. Then, in a second the whole scene changed. The elephants simply panicked: The sound that reverberated from deep within each animal told us of their anxiety and pain. In their stress they bumped into one another and even fell—not knowing where to go or what to do. Then an army jeep came around the corner and we thought we understood the reason for their distress. Even then we did not fully understand because there had been no poaching in Chobe for three years during which time the Chobe elephant population had increased to about 120,000—far more than one could expect from normal breeding. Jonathan believed that many elephants relocated to Chobe of their own accord. "We border Namibia, Angola, Zambia, and Zimbabwe," he says. "Elephants don't wait around when they hear the sound of gunfire. Here they have found peace."

It wasn't until the next day that we learned what had happened. Russell Crossey, our ranger from the Chobe Game Lodge (the venue for the remarriage of Richard Burton and Elizabeth Taylor), took us on a long tour of northern Chobe. On our return journey, close to the Zimbabwe border we saw ahead hundreds of vultures either gliding above the canopy of teak trees or watching from the branches. Russell surmised that we were likely to come across a lion kill. Instead we found a massacred breeding herd of elephants. They lay within a few yards of one another, their trunks cut off and discarded, and their lower heads, above their tusks, sawn off. It was a sight that left us numb with horror and sadness at the futility of the killing.

As soon as we were within radio contact with Chobe Game Lodge, Russell reported the poaching. The next morning at 6 a.m., we witnessed the infrastructure set up by Ian Khama: An extremely smart Botswana Army officer was waiting to debrief Russell. It did not take the army long to discover what had happened. They set up roadblocks and, using helicopters, found that a poaching team had come over the Zimbabwe border, probably in a jeep similar to that used by the Botswana Army. And even though the herd we had encountered the day before was 20 or 30 miles from the massacre, they seem to have known about it.

After dinner that evening we went onto one of the boats on the Chobe River and watched the stars and listened to the sounds of the night. We wondered at the incredible day, at the elephants and their caring. Where would they be in another hundred years? Although Botswana is making it clear that poaching is not tolerated, what about other countries in Africa? Would elephants there have a chance? We discussed the vision of a transfrontier park that would stretch from Etosha, in Namibia, past Chobe, the Victoria Falls, and Kariba, through the Zambezi Valley to Mana Pools in the east. This conservation initiative would give elephants, so symbolic of harmony in nature, free movement across a vast area of southern Africa. But how long will it take for this plan to become a reality?

IN NOVEMBER 2002 CITES (Convention on International Trade and Endangered Species) gave three countries permission to sell stocks of ivory: Botswana, Namibia, and South Africa. This was recognition that all three countries had gotten their house in order. Poaching is controlled and elephant populations have been on the increase. Two other countries, Zimbabwe and Zambia, were refused permission.

Chapter Six

Some Thorny Issues

*A*LTHOUGH BOTSWANA HAD TURNED THE CORNER IN THE 1980S, OTHER countries in Africa were heading in the opposite direction. Angola had gone to war. The Damara elephants in Namibia had been devastated when the South African military, led by its chief, Gen. Magnus Malan, used Damaraland as a hunting ground. Zimbabwe and Zambia were being drawn into a downward cycle of poverty and decay, and poaching was on the increase. Uganda had been through two decades of civil war that had all but destroyed the natural wealth of the country. Mozambique was struggling after decades of warfare, damage to the coastal plain caused by the Cahora Bassa dam—which restricted the flow of the Zambezi— and a series of cyclones that had brought floods and famine. Tanzania however, after a multiparty system of government was introduced in 1992, seemed on the road to becoming the wildlife mecca of Africa.

ABOVE: *Shells from the Indian Ocean* OPPOSITE: *The Zambezi River hurls itself over Victoria Falls.*
PRECEDING PAGES: *Lesser flamingos cluster in the shallow pan on the floor of the Ngorongoro Crater.*

The coral reef off the island of Zanzibar is home to a wide range of aquatic species from giant manta rays to beautiful devil firefish and deadly stonefish.

Tanzania

My path across the African continent has taken me on several occasions to Tanzania, and each time I crossed its borders I fell in love. It is a country brimful of natural beauty. It offers so much more than the grasslands of Serengeti and the Ngorongoro Crater, much more even than Kilimanjaro. The beautiful coastline, the coral reefs, Zanzibar and the offshore islands, the Rift Valley lakes, the many other mountains and volcanoes—some still active—the wild country of the Ruaha and Selous National Parks, and the shores of Lake Victoria and Lake Tanganyika combine to make this part of Africa incomparable.

For many years after independence, the socialist policies followed by the first president, Julius Nyerere, did little to advance private enterprise in Tanzania. Tourism was not a priority. Then in 1985 Ali Hassan Mwinyi became president and started a process of political and economic reform leading to the introduction of a multiparty system in 1992. From a slow start, the pace of expansion of the country's tourism industry picked up. It even seemed probable that Tanzania would follow Kenya in providing bargain-basement beach and bush safaris, thereby destroying the ambience that one comes to prize above all else when one looks back on a journey into the African wilderness.

In the 1990s another factor began to show itself. We called it the double-edged sword: the impact of too many people on an environment whose charm is its peace and quiet and whose magic is the biodiversity of life. From time to time I saw too many vehicles trying to follow a leopard or a cheetah on the hunt, too many planes overhead, too much noise, too much pollution, and too much damage to sensitive ecosystems.

One of the many safari operators to establish themselves in Tanzania in the 1990s was Conservation Corporation Africa. They rebuilt Klein's Camp at the source of the Grumeti River on the Kenya-Tanzania border, the Grumeti River tented camp in the western corridor of the Serengeti, and the Lake Manyara Tree Lodge in the Lake Manyara National Park. They also replaced the old Ngorongoro Crater Lodge with a series of small lodges so bizarre looking that when first seen through the swirling mists on the crater rim they might be mistaken for a scene from the tales of Rider Haggard.

From the moment I landed near Klein's Camp, I was spellbound. On the drive to the camp, named after Al Klein, an American who became one of East Africa's legendary professional hunters, we watched a leopard with its kill in a tree, about 30 giraffe running across the open grasslands, a pride of more than 20 lions relaxing in the shade, and a herd of elephants climbing the hillside above us. Although we had missed the main body of the migration, there were still vast herds passing by. Only my desire for a refreshing hot shower after a week on Kilimanjaro (anyone who has climbed Kilimanjaro will know how I felt) forced us off the plains and up to the lodge.

Klein's Camp—like Cottars 1920s Safari Camp just across the Kenya border—sits on land leased from the local Masai community. Les Carlisle, who was instrumental in the development of Phinda, talked about the relationship that has built up between CCAfrica and the Olosokwan community. "Klein's is such a magnificent area," he says. "On the one side we have the Serengeti National Park, on the other the community land, which acts as a buffer against inroads that poachers would like to make. The Masai are even using some of the lease money to employ game guards to protect wildlife on the land we lease from them. In return we're helping them with clinics, classrooms, and scholarships for their kids."

The Grumeti River, famous for the annual crossing of the migration and for its huge crocodiles, was also magnificent. There was just so much game that the lions sat in the shade on the riverbank and waited for a gazelle to pass by. There was no chase. Just a quick whack, and the lioness had her dinner. Lions are great opportunists, but I had never seen such blatant and confident behavior. One day everything seemed to grow on trees: trees full of pelicans, trees of colobus monkeys with their pretty white faces, trees of white egrets, trees of tree-climbing lion cubs. I felt like singing to the skies: "What a wonderful world!" We moved on to Lake Manyara Tree Lodge—a birdwatcher's paradise. Then on to Ngorongoro Crater, where wildlife and Masai cattle share limited space with many safari-goers.

Les Carlisle talked to me about Ngorongoro. "It's right here that you see in microcosm what can go wrong in Africa when you don't have controls," he says. "The crater floor extends over a relatively small area. In some respects it is an island—albeit a natural island without fences. Poaching is a problem, but as more and more Masai are involved in wildlife and benefit directly from it, I believe that poaching will reduce. Even more significant is the effect of tourism. The numbers of vehicles coming into the crater every day are just too many and are impacting heavily on this natural system.

"At the end of the year 2000 the Ngorongoro buffalo were dying. Researchers came in and were testing for disease. When I arrived I looked down at the crater floor. The wetland that had once been a green island was brown. When we got down onto the crater floor we found that a new hardened ring road had been built and drainage ditches had been cut under the road, not only channeling the water away from the road—good engineering— but also taking the water away from the wetlands and directly to the salt pans. The reed beds that would have sustained the buffalo through the dry season were dying. A further problem develops when drivers swing wide to avoid muddy puddles, until eventually the tracks become 60 to 70 yards wide. I believe that Ngorongoro has a limited window before the impact that man is making will lead to permanent change. Then people won't want to go there any more. We shouldn't let this happen."

I saw another example of poorly regulated tourism on Kilimanjaro, which is being climbed by more and more people each year. I remember the first time I caught sight of Kibo shimmering above the clouds in the early morning sun. Its beauty stunned me. When I climbed the mountain a few years later, we had terrible weather: rain, thunderstorms, hail, sleet, and a blizzard. But nothing destroyed the sheer splendor of the mountain. We heard elephants in the forest, caught glimpses of antelope, birds, and monkeys. The day before we reached the 16,000-foot-high saddle between the two peaks, Kibo and Mawenzi, a herd of buffalo had crossed over from Amboseli, in Kenya, onto the well-watered

TOP ROW: *Grey-crowned crane, Malachite kingfisher* CENTER ROW: *Female jacana, Crested guinea fowl* BOTTOM ROW: *Lilacbreasted roller, Ground hornbill*

eastern slopes of the mountain. I watched the dawn from the cave near the top of Kibo, where I had stopped, frozen and wet. Above me the blizzard was still blowing. Below me the mountain, well below the saddle, was covered in snow. Even Mawenzi, the lower peak, had snow clinging to its rocky face. And wherever I looked the red dawn over the Indian Ocean was reflected in that snow. I did not have a camera. I did not need one. It was unforgettable.

Many years later I visited Tanzania again and climbed Kilimanjaro a second time. What a difference. Global warming had caused the snow and ice to disappear, except for the glaciers at the very top. The elephants we had heard in the

LEFT: *Hippo slums may develop when water reserves run low.* FOLLOWING PAGES: *Bushbuck graze on grassy slopes soaked by billowing spray from the Victoria Falls.*

forests and the buffalo that had crossed the saddle ahead of us had long since gone. We did not see colobus monkeys. But we did see signs everywhere of the thousands of people that climb Kilimanjaro each year. Visitors are asked to leave nothing on the mountain, but it is not the practice. I could watch the long-tailed, scarlet-tufted malachite sunbird feeding on giant lobelias or look directly above at the towering majesty of the glaciers, but around every corner my eye caught sight of more and more garbage. When it rains, which is often, the paths act as funnels, channeling topsoil into the rivers and finally into the ocean, which as the crow flies is 200 miles away. It has recently been discovered that the coral reefs on the stretch of coastline where the Pangani River, which has its source on Kilimanjaro, reaches the sea are dying because they are covered in silt. If the reefs die all aquatic life will be affected and so will the fishing industry on which so many Tanzanians depend.

Nearly 40 percent of Tanzania's land is set aside for wildlife. The animals and birds are magnificent, and the open land-use systems are a great contrast to the isolated islands of wildlife elsewhere in Africa. The government is aware of the problems it faces and is adamant that it will not make way for mass tourism. But there is also a second scenario: overgrazing by Masai-owned cattle. The pastoral Masai still measure their wealth in cattle, and as benefits accrue from tourism, more cattle will inevitably compete for the already meager resources. This could escalate and result in a gradual desertification. Predators such as lions may slowly be wiped out because

of the threat they pose to cattle. As predator numbers diminish, the cattle and wildlife will thrive, accelerating the degradation of the habitat. No more animals. No more tourism. The threats are just as real as the opportunities, and monitoring the balance between them will be crucial in the years to come.

Zambia

My first stop in Zambia was Victoria Falls. In the dry months the falls are tame. Spectacular, yes, but lacking the awesome grandeur I saw as the Zambezi in full flood tumbled over the edge of the chasm. The thunderous roar of the falls was deafening. It made one realize how puny are human efforts compared with the forces of nature. It is not surprising that these falls, over 1 mile long and 355 feet high, are considered one of the natural wonders of the world.

Despite Zambia's natural wealth, much of the country's infrastructure has collapsed or is near collapse. My guide told me that he needed a PHD to drive in Zambia. I looked bemused. Then he laughed and told me that PHD stood for "pothole dodger." Worse are the abject poverty of the people and their lack of opportunity. There are organizations that are trying, with the government, to redirect the economy of Zambia, but it is not going to happen overnight.

Our destination on the banks of the Zambezi was Tongabezi, where we found a charming, quiet lodge. Our hosts, Ben Parker and his wife, Vanessa, like many other lodge owners in that part of Africa, were struggling. The international press coverage of Zimbabwe, showing white farmers being forcibly evicted from farms, has affected tourism in the whole region. Our conversations with the Parkers, on a deck overlooking the Zambezi, were frequently interrupted. Ben would stop in mid-sentence to point out a puffback in the trees above us, or African finfoot, spur-winged geese, or knobbilled ducks on the water. In the evening dinner was served on a wooden platform anchored in the Zambezi. With the galaxy of stars reflected in the waters around us and the plaintive song of a fiery-necked nightjar carrying from across the river, one could not imagine a more romantic setting.

Vanessa had started a small school for the children of the Tongabezi staff. Within a few years the number of pupils had risen to 105. There were many children starving for education in the local communities, and the nearest schools were at Livingstone, 12 miles away—a long way to walk, more so when you can't afford shoes. The school is funded by wellwishers from all over the world. It has secondhand computers and books from the UK, and a donated TV/video. As in many other places in Africa, lodges have the necessary infrastructure to help their

A lion cub quenches its thirst after gorging on a buffalo killed by the pride's females in Tanzania's Serengeti National Park.

neighbors. But the high costs of providing a 24-hour-a-day wilderness experience for guests as well as looking after their staff leaves little for funding clinics and schools. It is only because guests help support these projects that they survive.

Although Zambia's road network is in sad disarray, there is much that is very beautiful. The Kafue National Park has had its ups and downs over the past 40 years. Sometimes hunting has gotten out of hand, and at one stage, the herds of puku were devastated to provide food for the army. That changed, and the puku—which had been reduced to 10 percent of their population—have recovered. But there are no rhinos and only a few elephants left.

On the Busanga flood plain in northern Kafue we watched three cheetahs hunting. They had not seen the pride of lions ahead of them. We held our breath, but eventually, through the tall grass they saw the lions, which were by that time standing up and swishing their tails angrily. After a show of bravado, the cheetahs turned back to the nearby *vlei*, where they killed a reedbuck. The lions wasted no time in taking the kill from them, and the cheetahs would go hungry that day.

The expanse of the wilderness was astonishing. Sandgrouse came down to drink in the early morning, flapping their wings in the water and gathering moisture to take back to their nestlings. Kingfishers dived into the water to catch fish, and black-shouldered kites settled on the tall reeds to watch for the movement of some small animal. Our camp was entirely mobile. Everything that was brought in was taken out. The tents were small, and our dinner table had the added interest of a wood owl that watched us intently from the branch of an overhanging tree. Farther south, at the junction of the Lufupa and Kafue Rivers, the bird life was again spectacular. In the space of half an hour I saw several Pels fishing owls—one on a branch just above my head—Bohm's bee-eaters, and a pair of Ross's turacos, with their brilliant deep-blue and bright-red feathers. Anyone not hooked on birding would be captivated for life by this display.

To the east we had also visited the Chifungulu Camp in the Lower Zambezi National Park. Chifungulu is the African word for the sausage tree, *Kigelia africana*, which has deep-red trumpetlike flowers that dangle down from the tree and turn into the long cylindrical pods from which the tree takes its common name. We had a surprise waiting for us back at camp that first night: Elephants had taken over the camp, and we had to wait in our vehicles until they moved on.

The next day could not have been more peaceful. In the evening we watched a family of guinea fowl on a quiet backwater and just relaxed and listened to the sounds of the wilderness as the sun set. The guinea fowl were going about their business as usual when about a thousand European bee-eaters flew in and wasted no time in getting into their nests, dug into the bank opposite us. Their nests are about three feet deep and they must have been packed with birds, forcing the late arrivals to wheel around and fly off in great haste. It was almost dark by the time we got back to camp. Half an hour later we sat down to dinner under the canvas of an Arab-style tent. Then the wind started. By the time coffee came around it was impossible to pour the liquid out of the spout and into a mug—the wind was so vicious. We realized that the birds must have been aware that a cyclone was on its way. So, like the birds, we made haste to our beds. What a night! The wind howled. The rain thundered down, bringing branches and leaves into our "open to the sunshine" bathrooms. The next day all the elephants had gone. They did not want to be caught in the muddy riverine areas and had taken to the hills.

The North and South Luangwa National Parks have had a tumultuous history since being officially proclaimed in 1972. It is beautiful, wild country. But in the 1970s and 1980s poaching decimated the elephant population, and as many as 12,000 black rhinos disappeared. Poachers were so blatant that for a time it was not safe for travelers. Then in 1998 the Frankfurt Zoological Society signed a ten-year agreement to help finance a conservation project in the North Luangwa headed up by Hugh and Elsabè van der Westhuizen. This was followed up in 2001 with a moratorium on hunting, in an effort to control poaching. Now plans are in place to relocate black rhinos and increase the utilization of the park with community-owned camps on the border, as well as three more tourism sites within the reserve.

Zimbabwe

ZIMBABWE, WHICH COULD BE USING its natural resources to build a strong economy, is instead fast destroying the proverbial goose that lays the golden egg. The Victoria Falls Hotel still exudes the charm of its romantic history, but it is empty. The stunning Angola *pitta* still nests in the gorge near the top of the Zambezi escarpment in the Chizarira National Park. Further downstream on the Zambezi, Mana Pools, isolated from the troubles farther south, still has its spectacular wildlife. But the people of Zimbabwe are suffering. Even as this is being written, tourists are staying away. And where people are living side by side with game reserves, there are few animals left. Like Mozambique, Zimbabwe once attracted thousands of tourists. Right now all we can do is believe that for Zimbabwe this stage will pass, as it has for other countries in Africa that have had problems.

Uganda

FORTY YEARS AGO I VISITED UGANDA and was spellbound. In Murchison Falls National Park the hillsides covered in tall grass teemed with buffalo. We estimated there were about 5,000. The elephants, too, were everywhere—so much so that often we had to wait on the road for them to pass. The falls themselves were spectacular, and so were the crocodiles.

In the 1970s and 1980s Uganda was torn by a civil war that devastated many of the country's natural resources. There were few visitors in those decades. Today, after 15 years of stability, Uganda and its wonderful national parks are recovering. Tourists are going back to visit Murchison and the Nile, the mountain gorillas in the southwest, and the Queen Elizabeth National Park below the Mountains of the Moon. In Uganda it is evident, once again, just how quickly nature can rebuild given a helping hand.

FOLLOWING PAGES: *Inspired by Masai villages, the Ngorongoro Crater Lodge, built by CCAfrica, sits unobtrusively on the 8,000-foot-high rim of the caldera.*

Breaking Barriers

$\mathcal{E}$VER SINCE THE ARRIVAL OF MEN FROM EUROPE, BARRIERS TO CONSERVATION have been put up throughout Africa — perhaps in the Kruger National Park more than in any other region. Political ideology was the motivation for the erection of fences that cut the free movement of wildlife. The 7,529-square-mile park was closed to private enterprise, and agendas other than conservation were often perpetuated at the expense of animals. Decisions on conservation management were not always based on holistic thinking. And although conservation was key to unlocking wealth in the wilderness, rural people were largely cut off from its benefits. In the 1990s, step by step the barriers to conservation put up during the apartheid era

ABOVE: *Bushveld species flowers after a rain.* OPPOSITE: *Translocation and natural breeding have increased Addo's elephant population.* PRECEDING PAGES: *A barn owl is killed on a farmer's fence.*

started to crumble. The fences came down. Culling of elephants stopped. Species that had disappeared were reintroduced. And the practical way of utilizing the vast—and often untouched—wilderness was recognized: public sector-private sector partnerships involving rural communities.

The front-runner in this new era of cooperation was Ngala Game Reserve, bordering the Kruger National Park. In the early 1990s, soon after Phinda had gotten on its very wobbly feet, the privately owned Ngala Game Reserve was donated to the World Wide Fund for Nature (WWF). The management of the land was given to the Kruger Park, and CCAfrica was invited to build the first private five-star lodge within the Kruger Park. Even in those early years, CCAfrica had proved that it had expertise in the hospitality business as well as the ability to raise funds and work with rural people.

Nearly a decade later six areas within the Kruger Park were identified for private enterprise development—altogether covering about 2 percent of the Park. The Kruger Park was on its way into a new era: Kruger personnel could concentrate more on management of the wilderness, and private enterprise would take care of the upper end of the tourism market. One major break with the past was that, in terms of lease agreements, about one-quarter of the equity was reserved for black empowerment—including a stake for employees.

Luke Bailes, who had spent a decade making his Sabi Sand Singita lodges—according to the readers of *Condé Nast* "the best of the best"—was on the lookout for a location that would complement these existing lodges. At Singita, which means "place of miracles," he had set high standards in style and elegance. Luke found what he was looking for in the Lebombo region of the Kruger Park, where he won a 60-square-mile concession. At the confluence of the N'wanetsi and Sweni Rivers he built the Singita Lebombo Lodge, which, he says, "is so different from anything our guests have ever experienced." One feature of the region is its location at the ecological boundary between the tropics to the north and temperate climates to the south. In this transition zone there will always be birds that fly too far south or venture too far north. Or plants that flourish out of their normal zone.

The Lebombo mountain range was formed about 183 million years ago when fiery lavas of basalt and rhyolites were extruded through extensive cracks in the Earth's crust. The Lebombo range is part of our inheritance from that period. The volcanic extrusions have weathered, providing a nutrient-rich base for grasses and trees that attract the highest density of animals in the entire Kruger Park.

Among the staff at Lebombo are Julius Ngwenya and Piet Marimane, experienced rangers from the Sabi Sand reserves, and Dudu Mabunda, the first female

South Africa perfected the art of moving the planet's largest land mammal. Now elephant populations are springing up all over southern Africa—a fine example of the conservation offensive at work.

tracker in the industry. Julius, like his old colleague Sandros Sihlangu at Londolozi, has found his way through the obstacles to personal advancement put in his way during the apartheid years. Today he moves comfortably between his old world and the new, where he is able to converse authoritatively with international travelers. Together with other staff members, Julius is being given the opportunity to acquire an equity participation in Singita Lebombo, made possible through the Kruger to Canyons Biosphere Reserve Trust. It is a good investment for the staff. Luke has the recipe for success of a safari business: romance, excitement, and luxury. Julius is also an inspiration to other young Africans who, in the future, will host their country to the people of the world.

The Greater Limpopo Transfrontier Park

To the northeast of Singita Lebombo, a transfrontier park—a cooperation between three countries, Mozambique, Zimbabwe and South Africa—is under way. The extension of the Kruger Park east into Mozambique and north into Zimbabwe will create the 13,000-square-mile Greater Limpopo Transfrontier Park. The vast area to the east of the Kruger National Park once teemed with

wildlife. Then, during the Mozambique civil war, when the wildlife was killed to provide food and money for the army, it became a silent wilderness. The first elephants relocated across the Kruger border wasted no time in returning home, so, as a temporary measure to keep the relocated animals in, an electri-fied fence has been strung around a 100-square-mile area in Mozambique.

The Greater Limpopo is one of eight different transfrontier parks involving 232,000 square miles. The first transfrontier park came into being in May 2000 with the establishment of the Kgalagadi Transfrontier Park linking wilderness in South Africa and Botswana. Others are well on their way although some may take decades. What is important is that the vision of taking

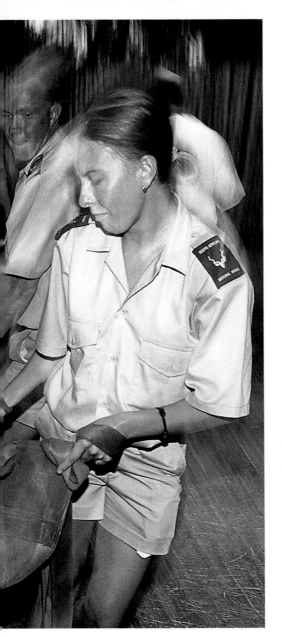

LEFT: *Kruger National Park staff prepare to inoculate a buffalo against tuberculosis.*
ABOVE: *A young elephant calf smiles at the world.*

down barriers that were arbitrarily put up a hundred years ago has been identified as vital to the sustainability of southern Africa's wildlife.

The next stage has already been set in motion: the repopulating of areas in southern Africa where wildlife has been devastated. The Kruger Park has developed into one of the finest custodians of the wilderness in Africa. Its research team is continually breaking new ground in its understanding of animal behavior and ecology and the management of the wilderness. Just three animals give proof of their ability: The elephant population increased between 1996 and 2002 from about 7,500 to over 10,500, and black rhinos and white rhinos, which were reintroduced to the Kruger in the 1960s, have now increased to about 500 and 4,000 respectively. Over the past decade more than a hundred rhinos have been transferred from the Kruger to zoos and game parks all over the world.

One of the major problems facing wilderness managers within South Africa is that most of the existing game reserves already have enough elephants, and it is generally acknowledged that some other means of controlling elephant populations must be found. At one stage there was hope that contraception would be the answer, but the cost and the trauma involved in darting the test female at six-monthly intervals was unacceptable. In addition, it was found that the hormones significantly changed the cow's relationship with the bulls. Because of her unnatural behavior, the bulls attacked the subadult males—all innocent bystanders that had not yet left the breeding herd.

Within the Kruger Park the elephants have caused considerable damage to the forests. Normally about 60 percent of an elephant's diet is grass. Have they turned to the forests because so much of the savanna grasslands have disappeared? Or are there simply too many elephants? The impact humans have made has changed the ecology of the region. As the water table has dropped, the grasslands have been taken over by the deeper-rooted acacia woodlands. Do we censure the elephants because they turn to the forests? Or do we first get our own house in order? Humans still have much to learn.

Relocating breeding herds and big bulls is no easy task. When an elephant is darted the relocation team has only a few minutes to move the massive animal onto its side before the pressure of its own weight crushes its heart and lungs. There is also the possibility that elephants may have an allergic response to the M99 capture drug or may suffer capture myopathy, a loss of muscle use. Since the Kruger Park veterinary and capture teams started moving elephants seven years ago, of the 750 relocated only 4 have been lost—a reflection of the teams' care and efficiency.

In December 2002 Dave Varty and Valli Moosa, Minister of Environmental Affairs and Tourism, watched the ceremonial breaking of the fence between the Kruger Park and Mozambique. For Dave it was a poignant moment: "It took me back to that first day I spent with Nelson Mandela at Londolozi over a decade ago. When he was president he had driven the conservation program forward and a lot of good things had happened in South Africa. Then Valli Moosa took over conservation and understood the Peace Parks vision. We should never underestimate his fortitude in breaking down the political barriers between the three countries. But he did. And in a relatively short time he has brought the transfrontier park into existence."

With the fence down it is unlikely that all 3,000 of the elephants destined for Mozambique will need to be relocated. Elephants have memories. They will

TOP ROW: *Water lilies, Wild gardenia* CENTER ROW: *Leucadendron, Leopard orchid*
BOTTOM ROW: *Giant carrion flower, Delagoa lily*

Mrs. Pretorius, whose husband, Maj. Jan Pretorius, was hired to kill all the Addo elephants

Hester, Blanche Emily, and Kate with family friends on the porch at Gorah

W HEN IAN HUNTER FIRST VISITED THE OLD FARMHOUSE AT
Gorah, he was captivated. It was here that man and
elephant had lived together in harmony for a century. Walking
through the ruins, a sixth sense told him that this was the site for the
development of a private lodge in the Addo. Here were memories and
ghosts of the past—ghosts of both people and elephants. The history
of Gorah revolves around two women who loved it and made it the
center of their lives: the matriarch, Hester Catherina de la Harpe,
and her niece, Blanche Emily de la Harpe.

Hester with her adopted son, Sydney

Harry Attrill, Hester's second husband

The old farmhouse at Gorah

Blanche and daughter Joy bottle-feed two baby elephants.

remember that to the east lay danger for the herds. But, with their ability to communicate (naturalist Katy Payne has proved that their "voices" carry about 18 miles), they will discover that others are enjoying the grasslands to the east, and with the fence down they will follow of their own accord. Dave Varty says: "Elephants are the great colonizers of Africa. Where they go other species will follow. They are such gentle creatures. Yet they bring energy and excitement, dynamism and change to sterile ecosystems. It just takes a little time." Dave speaks from experience. After the Kruger Park cut off the private reserves on its western boundary, there were few elephants in the Sabi Sand Reserve. In 2002, only six years after the fence was taken down, more than 600 elephants moved through the reserve.

Sheltering Plettenberg Bay from the southern winds, the Robberg Peninsula is a popular nature walk and site from which to view the whales that visit the bay by the hundreds each winter.

The Eastern Cape

ELEPHANT RELOCATION has been vital to the rebirth of the eastern Cape wilderness and to the tourism industry situated on what was once called the Quagga Plains inland from Algoa Bay. The history of this area goes back to the early days when the first settlers began to move north and east from Cape Town searching for well-watered farmlands and wealth. It was an arduous journey. In 1778, when the Dutch governor of the Cape, Baron Joachim van Plettenberg, visited the eastern Cape frontier, he agreed to provide protection for the frontiersmen who were caught in a war zone between opposing communities. Eight years later reference is made to the farm "de Gora," in the Khoisan language meaning a fountain or spring, and its owner, Commandant Daniel Willem Kuuhn.

With its dense bush and abundant water, the Gorah became known as a favorite haunt of elephants—perhaps more so when the elephants retreated into the adjacent Addo bush to escape men and guns. Hunting was probably more rewarding than farming in the early years. But it did have its dangers. One owner of the Gorah, Harry Attrill, was killed in 1900 when trying to capture an orphaned elephant calf. The matriarch appeared unexpectedly on the scene and charged. When Harry raised his rifle to fire, the bullet jammed in the barrel. The matriarch grabbed Harry with her trunk, first throwing him into the air and then crushing him under her feet.

In the 20th century more and more farmers moved into the area—especially after a major dam was built to irrigate citrus and other crops. The farmers eventually banded together and employed Maj. Jan Pretorius to exterminate all of the estimated 130 elephants remaining in the Addo bush. He managed to dispose of the majority before his contract ran out, but a few hid successfully from the hunter. Once again the government acted slowly, and in 1931, some years after Pretorius had departed, the Addo Elephant National Park was proclaimed. There were an estimated 11 elephants left, but none of them were within the proclaimed area!

Harry Trollope, who had spent three years in the Kruger Park with Col. James Stevenson-Hamilton, was called upon to help. His task was to drive the very dangerous and terrified elephants back into the Addo. It was a job that few men would have tackled. Frederick Courteney Selous is reputed to have said: "Going after elephants here is not hunting—it's suicide." The Addo bush was so thick that it was hard to find the elephants. Once they were found Harry's men had to drive them toward their new home without the elephants picking up their scent. If the elephants got so much as a whiff of men, they would charge. The last thing Harry wanted was to have to shoot elephants in self-defense.

Harry's strategy was to be very quiet, to use smoke to hide their scent and fire to persuade the elephants to move in the direction they had planned. His tactic worked, and before the end of the year the elephants were all in the proclaimed area—although they were far from settled and Harry was often called on to get them back when they broke out. A few years later an elephant-proof fence of railway sleepers was built around the reserve, and when counted there were nine adults and five calves. This group was the nucleus of the herds in Addo today.

In the late 1990s, at the suggestion of Michael Hodgen—grandson of Blanche de la Harpe, the adopted daughter of Hester and Harry Attrill—the Gorah farm was incorporated into the Addo. It was the start of a new era for this beautiful wilderness area in the Eastern Cape. Very soon thereafter the Cape Provincial Administration decided that if Addo was to achieve its full potential it would need partners in private enterprise. The Hunter family won the concession to operate a five-star ecotourism lodge at the Gorah. They surpassed their dreams when they took the ruined "de Gorah" farmhouse and restored it to the splendor and charm of a century ago. There could hardly be a more relaxing and charming way to get to know elephants than to watch them at the water hole from the Gorah patio or from your own private tented suite.

The next steps were to reintroduce elephants from the Kruger Park to create a greater gene pool and to incorporate adjacent land into the Addo. The vision is to establish an uninterrupted stretch of land all the way from the mountains to the sea. Riverbend Conservancy, one of Addo's neighbors, covers a 155-square-mile parcel of land, where restoration of the indigenous ecosystem and the relocation of game are under way. It will not be long before the fence between Riverbend and Addo will be taken down. When the plans for Addo are complete, visitors will be able to watch the elephants—now more than 400 strong —in the morning, and in the afternoon see the whales as they come into Algoa Bay to calve. It is a vision that is fast becoming a reality as the Greater Addo expands its borders to incorporate some 800 square miles of malaria-free wilderness.

The Pongolo Game Reserve

IN THE EARLY 1960s, while Lake Kariba, in what was then Rhodesia, was filling and its dam turbines rolling, the South African government drew up plans to build a dam on the Pongolo River in the Ubombo Mountains of Maputaland. They wanted to develop a giant irrigation scheme to grow sugar on the flood plain between the Pongolo and Mkuze rivers. Although the wall of the Pongolo River Dam—built on unstable ground—caused the civil engineers many headaches, the real problem with the construction lay downstream. The Pongolo River had been the lifeblood of the AmaThonga people for more than a thousand years. At the end of summer the floods renewed life on the numerous pans formed as the river meandered across the Maputaland flood plain. The dam destroyed far more than the AmaThonga's agricultural system, which relied on the seasonal ebb and flow of the river. It destroyed their way of life, their spirit, and their love of life. It also came close to destroying the ecology of the region. When the dam blocked the late summer floods, access channels to almost a hundred pans on the floodplain closed. This was the death knell for the tilapia and barbel, the water lilies and water chestnuts, the hippos and crocodile, and the birds. Everything was endangered, even the wonderful wetlands of the Ndumu Game Reserve. Only after a decade was it decided to simulate the natural flooding of the river by periodically opening the sluice gates wide. By that time much of the natural rhythm of the land had been destroyed.

The irrigation scheme also failed. During the 1970s an estimated 500,000 refugees from the war in Mozambique poured into the region. Many were AmaThonga, who settled easily among their own people. The logistics of moving such a vast number to make way for white farmers became unmanageable. As early as 1975 the government changed its mind. With export earnings sagging under the weight of international sanctions, it was decided to reserve the area for black development. The 50-square-mile dam was a complete white elephant.

There was one more twist to the tale. Heinz Kohrs was only a youngster when the dam was built, but his head was filled with dreams. He dreamed that one day he would qualify as a vet and work with animals. And he hoped that his father's farm—now on the shores near the Pongolapoort Dam—would have elephants. He told us: "I was about eight when I had a dream. I saw elephants on my father's farm. It was so wonderful that I was disappointed when I woke up. I wanted to go back to sleep to see the elephants again. I never forgot my dream, and when the opportunity came to join with our neighbors and form the Pongolo Game Reserve on the western shores of the dam, I did not hesitate. Our first family group of elephants arrived from the Kruger Park in 1997 and, with their arrival, we handed our farmlands back to nature."

With a little tongue-in-cheek humor, Heinz, now a qualified veterinarian, named the first camp on the shore near the Pongolo River Dam "White Elephant Safari Lodge." On the other side of the dam are the Lebombo Mountains in Swaziland and one of southern Africa's most notable archaeological sites. Border Cave has given up more than 69,000 Stone Age implements, and the remains of at least five *Homo sapiens* and 43 mammal species, including elephants, dating back 150,000 years. "We are on what I believe was an old elephant corridor," says Heinz. "We've even had elephants leave this reserve and walk 50 miles to the west to Mkuze Falls, another private reserve. Rather than shoot the elephants because they could have been a danger, we decided to use modern technology and collar them and let them go. We followed the bull to Mkuze Falls, where he spent several nights with a family group that had also been relocated from the Kruger. On his return he linked up with five orphans in yet another private reserve, 20 miles from here. Seven days later he was back. The next year, the five orphans came and paid him a visit—and stayed!

"We had wonderful support from the farmers who owned the land across which the elephants traversed. They saw it as we did—as a thrilling experience and probably normal elephant behavior. What was extraordinary was that elephants have not been here for well over a hundred years. And they were crossing electrified fences and traversing a rail line and main roads.

"We've also gone one stage further. We've set ourselves a target that by 2006 we will have reestablished the natural migration route of elephants through the Pongolo-Mkuze-Itala region. Our Space for Elephants conservation

Territorial stallions jostle for dominance at Itala Game Reserve, a keystone property in the development of a transfrontier park between South Africa and Mozambique and the reinstatement of an ancient elephant migration route. FOLLOWING PAGES: *Plans for the extension of Greater Addo Elephant National Park include a marine reserve. Attractions will include the big seven— elephants, rhinos, lions, buffalo, leopards, whales, and great white sharks.*

initiative has as its objectives the dropping of fences between private reserves and national parks, the extension of wilderness areas through the lease or purchase of land, and the negotiation of elephant traversing rights over community property with suitable compensation schemes. Space for Elephants Foundation also aims to assist with environmental education and boost the rural economy through the identification of small-business opportunities along the corridors."

The whole area is in transition. The 1,600-square-mile transfrontier park will include the Hlane Royal National Park and two adjacent reserves in Swaziland; Pongolo, Ndumu, and Tembe Reserves in South Africa; the Maputa Elephant Reserve in Mozambique; and the coastal plain, including the Kosi Lakes and Lake Sibayi. It is a mammoth land assembly and restoration project. It may even soon include Mkuze and Phinda. It will take time, but one day this "Zululand Elephant Coast" could be one of the great safari destinations of southern Africa.

Chapter Eight

The Conservation Offensive

"IN NATURE THERE ARE NEITHER REWARDS NOR PUNISHMENTS—THERE ARE consequences." This profound statement by Robert Ingersoll is perhaps the most important principle we have seen applied throughout this story. In our safari we have discovered how forgiving nature is and that given a helping hand she can mend herself. We have seen how the biodiversity of Africa is part of an intricate web that has evolved to complement a harsh continent. We have also learned that fences that reduce the mobility of wildlife are anathema. We have seen that water is the continent's most precious resource and that it is vital to protect catchments and wetlands. We have seen that good intentions, without a holistic understanding of the

ABOVE: *Tsetse fly* OPPOSITE: *Tall dunes at Sossiesvlei, in the Namib desert* PRECEDING PAGES:
For a brief moment, oryx leave their tracks on the Namib Naukluft Park's ocean of high dunes.

balance of nature, often end in disaster. And we have learned that Africa cannot continue on a destructive course—it needs to get back on a sustainable track.

The most exciting prospect for the future is that areas that had been cleared of animals can, within a relatively short time, once again buzz with life. In South Africa Ian Player showed that rhinoceros could be moved. Jan Oelofse, working in the Hluhluwe Game Reserve, discovered that a funnel made from opaque plastic curtains could be used for mass capture of antelope without injury and with little stress. Les Carlisle showed at Phinda that cheetah and lions could be successfully relocated. The wildlife technicians of the Kruger National Park developed the ability to capture and relocate the world's largest land mammal. Ian Craig and the

A Zulu woman's headdress of leopard skins shows that she is married to a man of stature.
FOLLOWING PAGES: *Male lions defend the pride and their territory from external aggression.*

Kenya Wildlife Department found a way to capture sitatunga in the swamps of Uganda. Nothing was easy. But the scene was set for creative conservation.

There is no doubt that conservationists in Africa are on the offensive. Each country has its own agenda. In South Africa top priorities are water conservation and removing fences. In Kenya and Tanzania it is controlling poaching and overutilization. In Mozambique and Angola it is establishing security for wildlife and getting animals back. In Zambia and Zimbabwe it is addressing poverty and reconnecting people to the benefits of the wilderness. With such people at the helm as Nelson Mandela, Thabo Mbeki, and Valli Moosa in South Africa, Ian Khama in Botswana, and Ian Craig in Kenya, who set in motion recovery and restoration projects, we have seen how much can be done. Many entrepreneurs are also making a major contribution toward utilizing the wilderness for the benefit of the land, the wildlife, and the rural people. In addition many rural people are putting land won under South Africa's redistribution program back under conservation, enabling them to be equity participants in the tourism industry.

In the long term nature will endure. But what of the short term? If we take too much water from the rivers and damage the catchment areas, the rivers won't run. If we apply inappropriate land-use practices, ecosystems will collapse and deserts will encroach. The consequences will be poverty, unemployment, and starvation—and the loss of biodiversity. Many people look at a map of Africa and presume that there is enough land to feed 840 million people and more. But how

many are aware that more than half the subcontinent is covered by desert? Added to that are the semiarid regions and places, such as the Chyulu Hills, that have been created out of porous volcanic lava that holds not a drop of water.

When John and Dave Varty worked with ecologist Ken Tinley, their hunting days ended and they found a way to repair the damaged habitat at Londolozi. Ken always said how important it is to think laterally. He reasoned that if one vlei dries up, everything that is water-dependent will naturally become extinct. If you take away the hippo, the grass gets longer. The wildebeest cannot eat or digest long grass, and they, in turn, will die out. In the meantime the buffalo population will expand because they prefer long grass.

LEFT: *Impala leap with grace and agility over distances of 12 to 13 feet.* ABOVE: *This pair of zebras, named Romeo and Juliet, spent day after day together, until eventually Romeo attempted to jump the fence and lost his life.* FOLLOWING PAGES: *Fig and fever forest at Mkuze, near Phinda Game Reserve*

Another thing we have learned is that the indigenous Africans have great wisdom to impart if only someone would listen. In the short time that Africa has been exposed to the more developed world, few people have understood or come to terms with the differences between Africa's nutrient-poor soils and haphazard rainfalls and the temperate climates of northern countries. Massive dams have been built with foreign aid, with many good intentions, to provide electricity and water for agricultural programs—for people who are pastoralists and on land unsuited to crop farming. Although many dams have created ecological problems and continue to fill uselessly with silt, some are being turned to recreational tourism with benefit to rural communities. One example is Kariba, a vast inland lake 175 miles long. When the dam was built on the Zambezi River, 50,000 people had to be moved and a mammoth project—Operation Noah—was set up to save animals trapped as the dam filled. Today much of the shoreline is the preserve of wildlife, including national parks,

reserves, and hunting concessions. Fishing earns important revenue for communities around the lake.

All too often in the 19th and 20th centuries, the people who used the wilderness were also its destroyers. That has changed. Today those who use the wilderness are in a unique position to be its custodians and to ensure that activities such as tourism are carefully controlled. African people, previously excluded from the benefits of tourism, are also finding opportunities—not just as trackers and rangers—but as managers, executives, and owners of ecotourism projects. It is fast becoming fact that conservation initiatives will succeed only if there is a genuine team effort involving all the stakeholders, including tourists who visit these areas.

In Africa the web of nature is readily apparent. We can watch the food chain, from the smallest insects to fearsome predators. We can see how species interact with one another. There are hundreds of symbiotic relationships from which each species gains an advantage in its struggle for survival. Edward O. Wilson, microbiologist turned conservationist, makes the point that planet Earth would manage very well without us. But could we manage without the millions of living organisms that ensure we have clean air and water and that our soil is renewed over and over again? Wilson suggests that there could be ten million or more species we know nothing about that are part of the planet's renewal process.

Africa needs us to come on safari and fall in love with her. Here we can watch a world that takes us far beyond ourselves and brings us to the realization of what we are doing to our planet. Dave Varty says: "For the past 250 years, since the industrial revolution, we have walked a path of extraction and destruction and are reaping the rewards. Global warming, worldwide terrorism, financial and economic woes are all part of our lives, as is the declining quality of life for both the rich and poor on this planet. A sixth great extinction, a worldwide epidemic of extinctions caused not by some catastrophic natural disaster but at the hand of man, is talked about as a distinct possibility. Yet here in Africa, where the diversity of Africa's wildlife is evidence of the extraordinary success of evolution, a new road is being taken—a road of restoration based on an Earth-centered approach to life: an understanding of community, of landscape patterns, and of the interconnectedness of all things. Africa is on a path of healing. It is to become more than a great adventure destination. It is where many will come to reconnect, to restore, and contemplate their purpose. Africa is the continent where, perhaps, we will find a course away from the sixth extinction. Come to Africa. See it. Feel it. Believe it. Because Africa belongs to us all."

TOP ROW: *Flap-necked chameleon, Tortoise* CENTER ROW: *Tinker reed frog, Foam nest frog* BOTTOM ROW: *Natal green snake, tiger snake* FOLLOWING PAGES: *Leopards gambol through the grasslands at Sabi Sand.*

Index

ÏNDΣℵ

Acknowledgments

I WOULD LIKE TO THANK THE FOLLOWING PEOPLE for their hospitality and for the many stories they shared with us: Calvin and Louise Cottar at their 1920s Safari Camp and Pat Cottar in Nairobi; Ian and Will Craig at Lewa Downs; Richard and Tara Bonham at Ol Donyo Wuas; Jonathan Gibson at Chobe Game Lodge; Ben and Vanessa Parker at Tongabezi; Luke Bailes at Singita; Christopher Kane-Berman at Londolozi; and Ian Hunter at Gorah.

There were also many people who helped me understand and see "their" corner of Africa: Colin Bell and Russell Crossey at Wilderness Safaris; Dr. Ian Player, founder of the Wilderness Leadership movement; Simon Blackburn at Singita Lebombo; Dr. Markus Hofmeyer of the Kruger National Park Game Capture Unit; Dr. Heinz Kohrs, co-founder of the Phongola Game Reserve and owner of the White Elephant Lodge; Pierre Delaney of KPMG; Les Carlisle of Conservation Corporation; Tony Dyer of the Professional Hunters' Association in Kenya; Ian Parker in Nairobi; Bongo Woodley, senior warden at Mount Kenya National Park; Julius Ngwenya at Singita; and Sandros Sihlangu at Londolozi.

I would also like to thank Richard du Toit and the other photographers; Ron West and Werner Bothner of Beith Electronic in Johannesburg, Shaun Mann for his valuable comments on the manuscript, Sandy Cunningham for directing our travels across Kenya, and editor Becky Lescaze for her clear understanding of what was right and what was wrong with the manuscript.

In particular I would like to give three people a very special thank you: Marilyn M. Gibbons of National Geographic, whose brainchild this book is, and Shan and Dave Varty, whose knowledge of the wilderness laid the foundation for this book and whose constant direction and advice kept me from wandering too far off track.

—Molly Buchanan

Illustrations

All images by Richard du Toit with the exception of the following: p. 6-7 Ariadne van Zandbergen; p. 24-5 Drawn & engraved by Samuel Daniell; p. 26 from the *London Illustrated News,* 1879; p. 27 François Levaillant; p. 29-31 (all) Samuel Daniell; p. 32 François Levaillant; p. 34-5 Samuel Daniell; p. 37 Captain Sir William Cornwallis Harris; p. 40-1 Samuel Daniell; p. 44 Museum Africa Archives, Johannesburg; p. 46-7 Courtesy Varty Family; p. 47 Spoornet Archives, Johannesburg; p. 48-9 Henry Lichtenstein; p. 51 Molly Buchanan; p. 52–3 (both) Kermit Roosevelt; p. 54 (up) Kermit Roosevelt; (lo) Cuninghame; p. 55 (up) Theodore Roosevelt; (lo) Kermit Roosevelt; p. 56 Edmund Heller; p. 57 Kermit Roosevelt; p. 59 (ctr, both & lo, both) Lex Hes; p. 62-5 (both) Heinrich van den Berg; p. 70 Marilyn Mofford Gibbons; p. 70-3 Roger de la Harpe/AfricaImagery.com; p. 74-9 (all) Courtesy Cottar Family; p 84 (up le) Ingrid van den Berg; (up rt, ctr le, & lo, both) Lex Hes; (ctr rt) ABPL Library; p. 88 Lex Hes; p. 90-5 (all) Courtesy Varty Family; p. 98-9 Gillian van Houten; p. 102 Philip van den Berg; p. 105 Heinrich van den Berg; p. 106-7 Rod Hastier; p. 107 Heinrich van den Berg; p. 109 (all) Peter Pinnock; p. 110-1 Roger de la Harpe/AfricaImagery.com; p. 118-9 Ariadne van Zandbergen; p. 120 Marilyn Mofford Gibbons; p. 135 (up rt) Heinrich van den Berg; (ctr, both) Philip van den Berg; p. 140-1 Ariadne van Zandbergen; p. 142 and 144 Roger de la Harpe/Africa Imagery.com; p. 147 (up, both & ctr rt) Heinrich van den Berg; p. 148-9 and 153 Ariadne van Zandbergen; p. 156-7 Roger de la Harpe/AfricaImagery.com; p. 160, 163, 164-165 Heinrich van den Berg; p. 167 (up le, ctr rt, lo rt) Lex Hes; (ctr le) Marilyn Mofford Gibbons; p. 168-171 (all) Courtesy Hunter Family; p. 172-3 Mike Allwood-Coppin; p. 178-9 Heinrich van den Berg; p. 182 Roger de la Harpe/AfricaImagery.com; p. 183 Lex Hes; p. 184-5 Roger de la Harpe/AfricaImagery.com; p. 190-1 CCAfrica; p. 193 (up le, ctr le, lo rt) Lex Hes

SAFARI

THE ROMANCE AND THE REALITY

Molly Buchanan

Published by the National Geographic Society

John M. Fahey, Jr.	*President and Chief Executive Officer*
Gilbert M. Grosvenor	*Chairman of the Board*
Nina D. Hoffman	*Executive Vice President*

Prepared by the Book Division

Kevin Mulroy	*Vice President and Editor-in-Chief*
Charles Kogod	*Illustrations Director*
Marianne R. Koszorus	*Design Director*
Barbara Brownell Grogan	*Executive Editor*

Staff for this Book

Marilyn Mofford Gibbons	*Project Editor and Illustrations Editor*
Rebecca Lescaze	*Text Editor*
Melissa Farris	*Art Director*
Carl Mehler	*Director of Maps*
Joseph F. Ochlak	*Map Research*
Matt Chwastyk	*Map Production*
Shaun H. Mann	*Contributing Editor*
Anne Withers	*Researcher*
Sharon K. Berry	*Illustrations Specialist*
Gary Colbert	*Production Director*
Richard S. Wain	*Production Project Manager*
Connie D. Binder	*Indexer*

Manufacturing and Quality Control

Christopher A. Liedel	*Chief Financial Officer*
Phillip L. Schlosser	*Managing Director*
John T. Dunn	*Technical Director*
Maryclare McGinty	*Manager*

Library of Congress Cataloging-in-Publication Data

Buchanan, Molly, 1934-
    Safari : the romance and the reality / Molly Buchanan
        p. cm.
    ISBN 0-7922-2765-4
    1. Big-game hunting—Africa—History. 2. Safaris—Africa—History.
    3. Nature conservation—Africa—History. I. National Geographic
    Society (U.S.) II. Title.

    SK251. B92147 2003
    799.296—dc22

                                            2003059336

One of the world's largest nonprofit scientific and educational organizations, the National Geographic Society was founded in 1888 "for the increase and diffusion of geographic knowledge." Fulfilling this mission, the Society educates and inspires millions every day through its magazines, books, television programs, videos, maps and atlases, research grants, the National Geographic Bee, teacher workshops, and innovative classroom materials. The Society is supported through membership dues, charitable gifts, and income from the sale of its educational products. This support is vital to National Geographic's mission to increase global understanding and promote conservation of our planet through exploration, research, and education.

For more information, please call
1-800-NGS LINE (647-5463)
or write to the following address:

National Geographic Society
1145 17th Street N.W.
Washington, D.C. 20036-4688
U.S.A.

Visit the Society's Web site at
www.nationalgeographic.com.

Composition for this book by the National
Geographic Book Division.
Printed and bound by R. R. Donnelly
& Sons, Willard, Ohio.
Color separations by Quad Imaging,
Alexandria, Virginia.
Dust jacket printed by the Miken Co.,
Cheektowaga, New York.